The Literary Agenda

Literature Against Fundamentalism

T0279986

The Literary Agenda

Literature Against Fundamentalism

TABISH KHAIR

OXFORD
UNIVERSITY PRESS

Great Clarendon Street, Oxford, OX2 6DP,
United Kingdom

Oxford University Press is a department of the University of Oxford.
It furthers the University's objective of excellence in research, scholarship,
and education by publishing worldwide. Oxford is a registered trade mark of
Oxford University Press in the UK and in certain other countries

© Tabish Khair 2024

The moral rights of the author have been asserted

All rights reserved. No part of this publication may be reproduced, stored in
a retrieval system, or transmitted, in any form or by any means, without the
prior permission in writing of Oxford University Press, or as expressly permitted
by law, by licence or under terms agreed with the appropriate reprographics
rights organization. Enquiries concerning reproduction outside the scope of the
above should be sent to the Rights Department, Oxford University Press, at the
address above

You must not circulate this work in any other form
and you must impose this same condition on any acquirer

Published in the United States of America by Oxford University Press
198 Madison Avenue, New York, NY 10016, United States of America

British Library Cataloguing in Publication Data

Data available

Library of Congress Control Number: 2024932911

ISBN 9780198919582

DOI: 10.1093/oso/9780198919582.001.0001

Printed and bound by
CPI Group (UK) Ltd, Croydon, CR0 4YY

Links to third party websites are provided by Oxford in good faith and
for information only. Oxford disclaims any responsibility for the materials
contained in any third party website referenced in this work.

Series Introduction

The Crisis in, the Threat to, the Plight of the Humanities: enter these phrases in Google's search engine and there are 23 million results, in a great fifty-year-long cry of distress, outrage, fear, and melancholy. Grant, even, that every single anxiety and complaint in that catalogue of woe is fully justified—the lack of public support for the arts, the cutbacks in government funding for the humanities, the imminent transformation of a literary and verbal culture by visual/virtual/digital media, the decline of reading . . . And still, though it were all true, and just because it might be, there would remain the problem of the response itself. Too often there's recourse to the shrill moan of offended piety or a defeatist withdrawal into professionalism.

The Literary Agenda is a series of short polemical monographs that believes there is a great deal that needs to be said about the state of literary education inside schools and universities and more fundamentally about the importance of literature and of reading in the wider world. The category of 'the literary' has always been contentious. What *is* clear, however, is how increasingly it is dismissed or is unrecognized as a way of thinking or an arena for thought. It is sceptically challenged from within, for example, by the sometimes rival claims of cultural history, contextualized explanation, or media studies. It is shaken from without by even greater pressures: by economic exigency and the severe social attitudes that can follow from it; by technological change that may leave the traditional forms of serious human communication looking merely antiquated. For just these reasons this is the right time for renewal, to start reinvigorated work into the meaning and value of literary reading for the sake of the future.

It is certainly no time to retreat within institutional walls. For all the academic resistance to 'instrumentalism', to governmental measurements of public impact and practical utility, literature exists in and across society. The 'literary' is not pure or specialized or self-confined; it is not restricted to the practitioner in writing or the academic in studying. It exists in the whole range of the world which is its subject matter: it consists in what non-writers actively receive from writings when, for example, they start to see the world more imaginatively as a result of reading novels and begin to think more carefully about human personality. It comes from literature making available much of human life that would not otherwise be existent to thought or recognizable as knowledge. If it is true that involvement in literature, so far from being a minority aesthetic, represents a significant contribution to the life of human thought, then that idea has to be argued at the public level without succumbing to a hollow rhetoric or bowing to a reductive worldview. Hence the effort of this series to take its place *between* literature and the world. The double-sided commitment to occupying that place and establishing its reality is the only 'agenda' here, without further prescription as to what should then be thought or done within it.

What is at stake is not simply some defensive or apologetic 'justification' in the abstract. The case as to why literature matters in the world not only has to be argued conceptually and strongly tested by thought, it should be given presence, be performed, and brought to life in the way that literature itself does. That is why this series includes the writers themselves, the novelists and poets, in order to try to close the gap between the thinking of the artists and the thinking of those who read and study them. It is why it also involves other kinds of thinkers—the philosopher, the theologian, the psychologist, the neuro-scientist— examining the role of literature within their own life's work and thought, and the effect of that work, in turn, upon literary thinking. This series admits and encourages personal voices in an unpredictable variety of individual approach and expression, speaking wherever possible across countries and disciplines and temperaments. It aims for something more than intellectual assent: rather the literary sense of what it is like to feel the thought, to embody an idea in a person, to bring it to being in a narrative or in aid of adventurous reflection. If the artists refer to their own works, if other thinkers return to ideas that have marked much of their working life, that is not their vanity nor a failure of originality. It is what the series has asked of them: to speak out of what they know and care about, in whatever language can best serve their most serious thinking, and without the necessity of trying to cover every issue or meet every objection in each volume.

Philip Davis

In memory of
JUSTIN D. EDWARDS
(1970–2022)

Acknowledgements

This book would not have been possible without a research grant from Carlsberg Foundation (Cheers!) and the patience and guidance of Professor Philip Davis and Eleanor Collins at Oxford University Press. A first draft of the book was efficiently tidied up by Madhula Bandyopadhyay, and I remain grateful for that. While I cannot list every friend or peer whose conversation has gone into forming this book, I do have to acknowledge the specific responses that I received on parts of two different chapters from Professor Susheila Nasta and Dr Anne Sophie Haahr Refskou, and on a section of the introduction and another chapter from the editors of *Berfrois* and the *Economic and Political Weekly* respectively. Thanks are also due to Dr Alexander Hardie-Forsyth at Oxford University Press for editing the final version of this book. Finally, a big hug to my family—Isabelle, Adian, Safia, and Alice—for tolerating my occasional remark at dinner on why reading literature is absolutely vital for humanity.

Contents

Introduction: What Is in a Word?

At the core of Anton Chekhov's short story, 'The Requiem', there is a tussle over a word.[1] Mass is just over in the small village church of Verhny Zaprudy. Andrey Andreyitch, a shopkeeper and an old inhabitant of the village, is angrily summoned by Father Gregory, still standing in his vestments by a door. He thrusts a small note at Andrey, demanding, 'Was it you asked for prayers for the rest of Mariya's soul?' In that note is written, in big, 'staggering' letters, 'For the rest of the soul of the servant of God, the harlot Mariya'. Andrey readily acknowledges that he had sent the note.[2]

Father Gregory is livid. It turns out that, unlike what the reader might have suspected, he is not angry at being asked to pray for a 'harlot'. How dare you write such a note, he asks? He knows that Mariya is Andrey's daughter. Andrey fails to understand the Father. For Andrey, his daughter, who had become a well-known actress in Moscow, is a harlot in Biblical terms.

Again, contrary to the expectations of some readers, Father Gregory is not really angry because Mariya is Andrey Andreyitch's daughter either. He has another reason, which allots a further significance to the word 'harlot', which he reads in a different context—a reading that Andrey cannot comprehend.

Despite using the word 'harlot', Andrey is praying sincerely for his dead daughter. 'But you know, the Lord in His mercy . . . forgave this very thing . . . forgave a harlot . . . ', he stutters in response. Father Gregory, on the other hand, is angry because he feels that Andrey is judging his dead daughter, while God has already forgiven her. He sees Andrey's use of the word as a 'sin', an act of over-subtlety. He

---

[1] An earlier version of my discussion of Chekhov's story appeared as an article that I published in *Berfrois* on 21 April 2021.

[2] Anton Chekhov, 'The Requiem', in *Best Short Stories of Anton Chekhov*, first published 1886, trans. Constance Garnett (Ahmedabad and Mumbai: Jaico Publishing House, 2018), 27–33, 28.

Literature Against Fundamentalism. Tabish Khair, Oxford University Press. © Tabish Khair (2024).
DOI: 10.1093/oso/9780198919582.003.0001

hectors Andrey, makes him do the penance of ten bows, and organizes a requiem in Mariya's memory. Andrey goes back to the pews and thinks of his last meeting with his daughter, a small girl he had not even noticed growing up into a young woman, while he was so busy working as a lackey for the rich. It is these rich people that, out of boredom, had taken the pretty and intelligent young girl in hand, and brought her up with lady-like grace, which had finally enabled her success as an actress.

Andrey thinks of how, three years before her death, Mariya had visited him. He had hardly recognized her. A graceful, elegantly dressed young lady, she talked cleverly, 'as though from a book'. Just before leaving, she had asked her father to accompany her for a walk along the river. There she had spoken enthusiastically about the natural beauty of the riverside, while Andrey had remarked that the space was simply being wasted, not understanding his daughter's enthusiasm. Mariya had burst into tears, and 'she had cried and cried, drawing her breath greedily with her whole chest, as though she felt she had not a long time left to breathe'.

As the singing continues in the village church, Andrey shakes his head 'like a horse that has been bitten ... to stifle painful memories'. Then he prays for his daughter: 'Be mindful, O Lord, of Thy departed servant, the harlot Mariya, and forgive her sins, voluntary or involuntary ... '. He does not notice the 'unseemly' word drop from his lips, for no exhortation from Father Gregory can drive out what is firmly embedded in his conscience. The short story ends with a beautiful description, slow, sad, and alive, of coils of smoke ('like a child's curls') drifting up from censor across a slanting patch of sunlight.

I hesitate to 'theorize' about this story, just as I hesitate to theorize about any good work of literature, for it often means channelling literature into another discourse. This is not an 'anti-theory' statement, as hopefully will become clear in this book, but it is based on a reluctance to mediate the language of literature through another language-use, often, in many academic versions, reducing it to secondary importance. Hence, I hesitate to bring in over-crusted terms, like 'perspective', 'generation', or 'class', though in due course I will. I feel like I am doing violence to the story if I even say, for instance, that the story is about the differences between Andrey and Father

Gregory, and between Andrey and Mariya, both unsurmountable, both containing a degree of care and, in the case of the relationship between father and daughter, genuine love. One of the reasons why I feel any statement like this does violence to the story is that the story itself never puts it in words. The words in and of the story themselves can be misleading: Can a father who calls his daughter a 'harlot' actually love her?

But it is exactly, I would argue, because Chekhov does *not* put this and other matters in words that we encounter them with a force that leaves us stunned. To reduce this 'silence' to a cluster of words—theoretical, critical, or explanatory—seems to impose a heavy degree of paraphrasing that, no matter how necessary or even accurate in a certain context, will nevertheless be reductive. Or, at its simplest, as a novelist must feel when asked what his new novel is 'about': 'Why should I have written 300 odd pages if I could tell you that in a few lines? Why should I use another language to talk about what happens in and outside language in my novel?' And, in this context, it is not insignificant that the story hinges around a 'note', which contains a certain word (harlot) that obviously carries the same *and* different meanings for Andrey and Father Gregory.

It is not as if both of them do not understand the dictionary meaning of the word, but even this meaning is not sufficient. The word has different associations for them and they relate differently to the person the word has been attached to. In this sense, they are like readers—not only do they approach the 'primary' text from different perspectives, they also approach it with different experiences of the world and other texts. As Charles E. Bressler puts it: 'Our response to any text, then . . . is largely a conditioned or socially constructed one; that is, how we arrive at meaning in fiction is in part determined by our past experience'.[3]

But the matter is more complex than that. For instance, it is significant that Chekhov employs a word, 'harlot', whose meaning is largely clear and evidently shared by both Andrey and Father Gregory. In the context of the story, it is not an ambiguous word. It is not its meaning which is in question, but its significance.

[3] Charles E. Bressler, *Literary Criticism: An Introduction to Theory and Practice*, first published 1994 (New Jersey: Prentice Hall, 2003), 6.

Literature and God

What Chekhov's story reveals is that the *significance* of the meaning of a word can vary from person to person, position to position. Significance, even though it is defined as a synonym of 'meaning' in dictionaries, comes from a different source, 'sign', than meaning. A sign is not a meaning, but a gesture or a mark to convey a meaning. The Latin signum stands for mark or token. Meaning, on the other hand, comes from mean, which stresses understanding and communication: 'have in mind, intend, import'. Its source word in Old English and Old Saxon (mênian) stood for 'intend' and 'make known'. In other words, something can have significance without it being communicable, and something that is not communicable cannot be 'intended' or 'made known'.

If the 'word' is considered the smallest unit of verbal meaning, then the notion that the word was with God and that the word was God is a recognition of the fact that literature and God began as Siamese twins. The unuttered utterance—the word with God—is seen as the source of creation: when God speaks it into being. But this uttering of the word is also literature. All religions have versions of this, and they subsequently insist on the fact that their revealed or sacred texts are the best of literature.[4] (Here I am avoiding, for the time being, the matter of all known languages being, from a scientific perspective, human constructs, and hence the 'revelations' of God being, at best, a matter of translation, with all the dangers attendant on translation.)

But what happens to the 'word' once it has been uttered, once it is no longer with God, once it is no longer God? Note that the following problems crop up even if we do *not* dismiss the existence of God—and, obviously, they are also there when we do.

The 'word', so to say, has entered the realm of humans, and (for the religious) it needs to be protected from human contamination. In different ways, early religions have resisted the profane proliferation

---

[4] I am not talking of academic scholarship, but of lay and sometimes institutional positions, as, for instance, among the majority of shariah scholars and various religious clergies. In terms of academic scholarship, there has been, particularly in recent years, a growing study of the overlap between the creative imagination and religious writing. Entire journals, such as *Literature and Theology* and *Journal of Religion and Literature* are devoted to this. I have refrained from entering this larger area, in order to confine myself to the points I wish to highlight about literature as an antidote to fundamentalism.

of their sacred texts. This is not confined to just the trinity of Judaism, Christianity, and Islam, with their 'revealed' and written literatures. Brahminical Hinduism even resisted the writing down of the earliest sacred texts, preferring the method of oral transmission from one 'pure' Brahmin to another 'pure' Brahmin. It needed the anti-Brahminical revolutions of Buddhism and Jainism—largely artisanal and 'middle' class/caste movements in their early years—to institute the written text as a mode of transmission. This was probably not just because of their 'artisanal' and 'merchant' following (which implies some secular literacy and writing) and their suspicion of Brahminism, but also because their adherents were initially spread thinly over a large expanse and did not have the institutional network of Brahminical Hinduism. In any case, even though they predate them by centuries in oral forms, it appears that major Brahminical Hindu texts started being extensively written down—and not transmitted orally—after the example and challenge of Buddhist and Jain texts. Despite this, the Brahminical preference for oral transmission continued for centuries.

The overlap between literature and God slowly thins out as the 'word' of God is crafted by not just human mouths, for mouths are easily controlled, but also by human hands and eyes: the ability of the written word to escape imprisonment is legendary. But it is not just imprisonment that the written word can escape. It can escape control—control over meanings. The religious way out of this—such as in the 'theology of accommodation', which says that though God is absolutely unknowable, He allows Himself to be accessed relative to human terms in translation—does not get beyond the issue of translation, best encapsulated by Emily Apter's twenty theses on translation. The first and last of these theses posit that nothing in translatable and that everything is translatable, with eighteen other permutations in between.[5]

The ability of the written word to escape imprisonment is not a new point: much of M. M. Bakhtin's relevance to the study of the novel rests on and develops from it.[6] Bakhtin is often read as highlighting

---

[5] Emily Apter, *The Translation Zone: A New Comparative Literature* (Princeton and Oxford: Princeton University Press, 2006), xi–xii.

[6] M. M. Bakhtin, *The Dialogic Imagination*. Ed. Michael Holquist, trans. Caryl Emerson and Michael Holquist (Austin: University of Texas), 1981.

polyvalence and multiplicity of the word, but his focus is on language in writing, not on primary orality: this is a matter I will examine in the chapter, 'Language, Literature, and the Book'. Or, as the speaker in Tony Harrison's great elegy puts it, after seeing 'UNITED' (signifying a soccer team) sprayed on his parents' gravestone in Leeds by a skinhead 'pissed on beer':

> [. . .] it's hard not to make
> a sort of furtive prayer from this skin's scrawl,
> his UNITED means 'in Heaven' for their sake [. . .][7]

Of course, this 'accident of meaning' in Harrison's poem is possible only because 'UNITED' has been written down, as Bakhtin would have immediately noted. 'This pen's all I have of magic wand', writes Harrison at the start of this passage of description, and actually the skinhead's spray-can is also a magic wand of sorts, because, like Harrison's pen, it *writes* 'UNITED' on the gravestone. Andrey and Father Gregory have an even more complicated (mis)understanding (over) of a word ('harlot'), whose meaning both of them know. Once again, it is a written word. It is such gaps that the written word introduces or exacerbates that enable the reader to go beyond the 'intention' of the author. Moreover, as we shall see later, 'God' as a word is itself a signifier with an undefinable, indeterminate signified, a sign with no exact or exhaustive referent. It is one of those words where the arbitrariness of representation—and hence the mutability of meanings and significances—is particularly pronounced. It requires a reading of not just what is stated, but also *what is not stated* and *cannot be stated*.

Therefore, I argue in this book that literature calls for an 'agnostic' reading, that actually reading *literature as literature*[8] trains us in this activity, and that this activity is not just an antidote to fundamentalism

---

[7] Tony Harrison, *V. and Other Poems*, first published 1984 (New York: Farrar, Straus and Giroux, 1990), 7.

[8] It is true, as one sociologist puts it, 'that many people *doing* art, *doing* music, *doing* drama, *doing* literature, not just consuming it, is an extraordinarily powerful mode for both solidifying commitment to social movements and for helping them achieve their goals'. (William G. Roy, 'How Social Movements Do Culture', *International Journal of Politics, Culture and Society*, vol. 23 (2010), 85–98, 86, or. ital.). 'Doing' literature also has various personal uses, not least that of expressing oneself that MFA courses capitalize on. But this does not define literature or exhaust it. To say so is not to say anything that is not widely accepted in other fields. For instance, many of us can knock together

(religious, political etc.) but also an essential, and increasingly overlooked, aspect of living in the world for human beings. Note that this claim does not reduce the scope to literature: I do not claim that only what we call literature demands this; I claim that all texts that demand what I will illustrate as 'agnostic' reading are literature. I need to stress, sometimes even with a degree of repetition, this characteristic of literature, before I can illustrate why and how literature is an antidote to religious (and other kinds of) fundamentalism.

The Chapters that Follow

In general terms, this book is based on an evident idea that I have developed elsewhere and do not dwell upon in detail here, for it is not necessary: that literature is a mode of thinking, stories being perhaps the oldest thinking 'device' known to humankind. The ways in which literature enables us to think are distinctive and necessary, because of the relationships between its material ('language') and its subject matter ('reality', internal, external or both). These relationships are exposed in their fullest complexity with the rise of literature as writing (and not just as any writing)—and, hence, this book looks at the book too, distinguishing between oral and written literatures without dismissing the former or subsuming the latter. I argue that literature enables us to engage with reality in language, and language in reality—where both are mutually constitutive, constantly changing, and partly elusive. This mode of engagement, I set out to show in this book, is essentially an agnostic one. Hence, it should be clarified, as is indicated by the title, that this is not a book on fundamentalism *and* literature: it does not present a study of how fundamentalism has been narrated in exciting literary works such as Salman Rushdie's *The Moor's Last Sigh* (1995) or Mohsin Hamid's *The Reluctant Fundamentalist* (2012). That is not my concern, and there are already books and anthologies that do so.[9]

---

a bird house or even a stool, but we are not carpenters, and all of us indulge in some self- and family medication, but we do not claim to be medical doctors. It is only in the liberal arts that necessary democratic credentials seem to be stretched as a rule into sheer demagogy. Hence, I insist on the distinctiveness of literature, and try to establish it in the book.

[9] See, for instance, Catherine Pesso-Miquel and Klaus Stierstorfer, Ed., *Burning Books: Negotiations Between Fundamentalism and Literature* (New York: AMS Press, 2012).

The chapter after this one is titled 'What Literature Does Not Say'. It makes the argument, already outlined in my reading of Chekov's story in this chapter, that literature is not just about language, though of course it cannot exist without language. I do not claim that this is an original argument: almost all major scholars of literature, at least from the middle of the twentieth century onwards, have been aware of it, though sometimes they have not developed the argument further or simplified it into regimented methods and terms, which inevitably have their limits. Hence, I do not set out to specify with terminology or methodology all the ways in which literature uses language as necessary and insufficient: such a transparent listing of what literature does would be, in keeping with my thesis here, a misreading of literature. Extreme transparency (as in Google reviews) is just as much of a misreading of literature as can be a relentless use of obtuse terminology, which can turn literature into a textual version of the subaltern who cannot speak, for some of the reasons that Gayatri Spivak gave in order to argue, in her seminal essay, that the subaltern cannot speak.[10] Actually, both run the risk of replacing literature with something else, at best only one of its aspects. Instead, I will look at certain texts, and suggest how and why they say more than the language of their expression, and why a summary of what they say or do not say, as in the case of the Chekhov story, might be necessary in university departments, but is actually a misreading of literature.

This chapter is followed by two others that look more closely at the matter of 'gaps' and 'silences' in the language of literature, and how these constitute literature just as much as its explicit language does. In these two chapters, 'Literature, Gaps, and Historicity' and 'Literature, Gaps, and Ahistoricity' by providing a reading of Mark Twain's *Huckleberry Finn* and William Shakespeare's *Hamlet*—both slanted differently across the historical, social, political, etc.—I further examine how and why literature goes beyond what can be said, or even what could be said. Implicit in the discussion is a differentiation between fiction and 'fake news', one that applies not just to literature but also to its reading, and, to my mind, enables us to answer the question of good

---

[10] Gayatri Spivak, 'Can the Subaltern Speak?', in *Marxism and the Interpretation of Culture*, eds. Cary Nelson and Lawrence Grossberg (Urbana and Chicago: University of Illinois Press, 1988), 271–313.

and bad readings of a literary text that bothered even a 'postmodern' novelist-critic like Umberto Eco. I could have selected a hundred other texts for this illustration, and I also make no claim that my illustration comes close to exhausting the matter under discussion. It is just an example. Given the nature of my argument, I choose to present readings of texts as illustrations instead of setting out critical tenets—a process that I suspect would be liable to promote critically 'fundamentalist' readings of literature, and hence produce a relative failure to read literature. It is exactly this failure that my book warns against, and connects to a larger failure in reading the world—one that is most dramatically illustrated by religious fundamentalists, with their refusal to read literature as literature, but is not simply confined to them.

Until now, to my mind, the matter has been simple, and not controversial, except for those who want to reduce literature to the sort of fundamentalist clarity that actually belongs to propaganda. Those of us who read literature as literature have long known to look for the gaps and silences between its words and lines, and theory has addressed aspects of it in different ways, ranging from feminist,[11] Marxist,[12] and post-colonial[13] re-readings and Edward Said's concept of contrapuntal reading,[14] through the various permutations of deconstruction[15] and post-structuralism,[16] and to the very idea of reader response theories.[17] I differ from this varied train of extant realization mainly to the extent that I insist on using the gaps and silences to adumbrate—formulate is not a word I would use—a definition of literature as literature, which is essential to proving that it is the antidote to fundamentalism. In short, it is not in what is said or can be

---

[11] Sneja Gunew, Ed., *A Reader in Feminist Knowledge* (London and New York: Routledge, 1991).

[12] Pierre Macherey, *A Theory of Literary Production* (1978) Trans. by Geoffrey Wall (London and New York: Routledge, 2006).

[13] Elleke Boehmer, *Colonial and Postcolonial Literature* (Oxford: Oxford University Press, 1995), and Bart Moore-Gilbert, *Postcolonial Theory: Contexts, Practices, Politics* (London: Verso), 1997.

[14] Edward Said, *Culture and Imperialism* (New York: Vintage Books), 1993.

[15] Jacques Derrida, *Of Grammatology*. Trans. by Gayatri Spivak (Baltimore and London: Johns Hopkins University Press, 1976).

[16] Benoit Dillet, Robert Porter, and Iain Mackenzie, Eds. *The Edinburgh Companion to Poststructuralism* (Edinburgh: Edinburgh University Press, 2013).

[17] Wolfgang Iser, *The Act of Reading: A Theory of Aesthetic Response* (Baltimore and London: The Johns Hopkins University Press, 1978).

said in language that literature becomes literature; it is in what is not said and sometimes cannot be said in language. While gaps, silences, turgidity, and 'deference' may be a condition of language in general, literature approaches and uses this condition in a distinctive manner. Neither are gaps and silences secondary to an understanding of literature, just one of its many aspects, as they are usually made out to be. They are *central* to its definition. But now, with the next chapter, 'Language, Literature, and the Book', we look at exactly how and why literature both uses and goes beyond language. In the process of doing so, we also look at literature as the written, and not the spoken, word, and the relationship between these two. Our discussion of language in the world brings us to one of the core issues—and strengths—of literature: how do we talk about what does not exist, at least materially in our world? This endeavour is complicated by the fact that literature often also talks about what might exist in other worlds but does not exist in the world of the reader—or even the writer. For instance, most of us have not seen a murder or a rape or, for that matter, a war. In some ways, we have not seen or experienced anything ever described in a work of fiction, or by another person: my experience of even my divorce will be, per force, different from someone else's narration of her divorce. Then, in the next chapter, 'Fundamentalism, Literature, and God', we essentially look at the ways in which the signifier 'God' when read in literature or as literature is anathema to fundamentalism. This brings us back to the agnostic reading that I repeatedly stress is inculcated by literature and that is an essential and necessary mode of understanding human existence.

Given the nature of this book, it should be stated at the start that I am not formally religious and do not believe in a God—or 'Force' or 'Being' or 'Spirit' or 'Power'—that can be manipulated, propitiated, flattered, pleased, or influenced in any way. Neither do I believe in a God that exists to take interest in human affairs, or the universe. In that sense, I will be termed an atheist, but that is a term I do not apply to myself either. The reasons for this I discuss in this chapter, which also presents my understanding of what is often called 'God'. It develops that understanding—in which I actually argue that an agnostic concept of 'God' is inevitable for human thought—into an understanding of fundamentalism, which is finally a totalizing insistence on pinning down in language what cannot and will not be reduced to language. In an obvious way, also conceded by some branches of religious thinking, this is applicable to 'God'. But in a less obvious way, it is applicable to all of the world, in which language both exists and whose existence language also impacts upon. I argue that the fact that we exist in and by language, that we can neither be reduced to language nor escape it—except as fundamentalist diktats—creates a bid to pin down 'reality'. This is fully justifiable, on many grounds, including that of communication: how can we discuss matters at an equivalent level unless words, often reduced to terms, are pinned down to specific meanings? However, this is also at the same time an impossibility.

My argument in this book is simply that literature is a particular use of language that works with, and not against, the essential slipperiness of the mutual relationship between language and reality, and in this sense it differs from other disciplinary uses of language, and that the discipline of literary studies, no matter whether it is liberal humanism or postcolonialism, often fails to address literature precisely because of its insistence on disciplining it. It is also exactly in this sense that literature as literature is an antidote to not just religious fundamentalism but also all other kinds of fundamentalism.

My discussion in this book obviously assumes a position on language, while avoiding the profusion of terminology and jargon that an academic involvement—which is not necessary here—would precipitate. This position is framed by Ferdinand de Saussure's definition of language as an arbitrary system of differences.[18] At its simplest, we know that philosophers had long suggested that there is nothing natural linking the sign to the referent, that, in other words, Adam did not just 'give' things their natural names. Neither, to move to another tradition, was a language especially in tune with the reality discussed: 'Many Sanskrit words and phrases are traditionally said to evoke and vibrate in tune with the nature of the qualities they name'.[19] With Saussure dividing the sign into signifier and signified, this matter got more obvious. There was no natural link between the signifier and

[18] Ferdinand de Saussure, *Course in General Linguistics*. Eds. Charles Bally and Albert Sechehaye, trans. by Wade Baskin (London: Fontana, 1974).

[19] Cleo Kearns, 'Hinduism', in Susan M. Felch, ed., *The Cambridge Companion to Literature and Religion* (Cambridge: Cambridge University Press, 2016), 151–68, 153.

signified either. Meaning in language came about because of a system
of differences: 'Concepts are purely differential and defined not by
their positive content but negatively by their relations with the other
terms of the system. Their most precise characteristic is in being what
the others are not'.[20] Or, put simply, the signifier-stool was not what
it was because there was a natural link between it and the signified-
stool, but because of a system of differences between stool, chair, sofa,
bench, table, etc. as signifiers. Hence, the obvious point that language
is a system of differences and does not arise out of a direct reflection
of 'reality out there'. There is always, so to say, a gap.

What, however, often tends to get forgotten in the discussion is that
Saussure's definition also posits a relationship, though still arbitrary
and not natural or direct, between language and 'reality out there'.
That is so because any change in a system of differences has effects
elsewhere in that language. So, if 'stool' were to disappear from English, it would affect the meaning of one or more of other signifiers,
such as 'sofa', 'chair', etc.[21] Hence, the Saussurian position on language does not divorce language from 'reality', leaving us nothing
but 'idealist' words to play with; it actually increases our awareness
of the many gaps, silences and shifts that exist within the system of differences that is language, and between that system and the arbitrary
but not unrelated world outside language, the world which language
shapes or maybe even produces *for me* and of which it is also a product
with and without me. I suggest in this book that the full import of this

---

[20] Saussure, *ibid.*, 117.

[21] This perception can be expanded from signifier/signified to sign/referent in a similar way. As someone born in Hinduism-dominated India, I have always been aware of
this. For instance, Sarasvati is first mentioned as one of the major (deified) rivers of India
in the Rig Veda and the other Vedas, and then mentioned as a minor river in later post-
Vedic texts. In actual fact, despite various efforts, there exists no river in contemporary
South Asia that can be identified as Sarasvati. In short, while Ganges or Sindhu (Indus)
is associated with a flow of water 'out there', no such flow of water is adduced to Sarasvati. Hence, the sign Sarasvati has no referent in the material reality 'out there'. But this
does not mean that it can be erased, because its existence as a sign (signifier/signified)
effects various things out there, including the meanings and significances attributed to
Ganges, Sindhu, etc. Hence, while any signifier/signified and any sign/referent do not
have a natural link and are arbitrarily yoked together, as a system of differences language is not totally a haphazard play and, most significantly, it is both effected by and
affects the 'reality out there'. The easy way out that some postmodernists found, by
reducing everything to a play of language, is simply not available to us, or at least not
available except as a serious version of a party game.

complex relationship is explored in and by literature, and denied by all kinds of fundamentalism.

The concluding chapter, 'A Call to Literature' looks at what literature does, this time in the light of the controversy between the humanities and science, where the former mostly comes out thoroughly battered or heavily defensive in other accounts. While staying focussed on literature, it argues that the humanities deal with highly mutable realities, and hence cannot offer the predictability of the sciences: for instance, the human genome hardly changes compared to the high and fast mutability of a language. This, and related matters, are essential to understanding what literature does, and why the agnostic reading demanded by literature is not a choice or a fad, but a necessity. This final chapter also ties together the loose ends of my arguments and argues that the ability to read literature *as* literature is crucial to our survival as a distinctive species of sentient beings. The reader is best allowed to access that argument in full, and not via a reductive—or even, alas, a potentially fundamentalist—summary here. In general, my argument in this book precludes an easy itemization of its points, for that would be to do exactly what I argue an agnostic reading trains us not to do. However, as I hope will become clear to the reader as my argument rolls out and sometimes returns to certain points from other angles, an agnostic reading is also not an abandonment of the activity of reading—or of making sense of the text and, through the text, of what we often call reality.

1

What Literature Does Not Say

The general idea that human beings are 'storytelling' animals is now widely pervasive, particularly following the popularity of books by Yuval Noah Harari.[1] I have made a similar connection when I noted, in the previous chapter, that religion and literature began as twins: whatever may be the nature or existence of divinity, rituals etc. in different religions (and these vary widely), there is no doubt that all of them are accessed by us (and the devout) through stories. But I do not want to stop at this level: stories might be common to all of human consciousness, but they operate in distinctive ways in literature.

One way to approach this would be to address the trajectory of stories in anthropology and in literature, a difference that is pertinent to what I call the agnostic reading of literature. This difference has to be illustrated because literature does not simply work by providing 'thick description',[2] as contemporary anthropological writing often provides even thicker description, without having the effect of literature, except in cases, such as Amitav Ghosh's *In an Antique Land*, where the anthropologist clearly and decisively embraces the techniques and ethos of literature. For instance, in *The Mushroom at the End of the World*, Anna Lowenhaupt Tsing stresses the 'scientific' value of stories: 'To listen to and tell a rush of stories is a *method*.'[3] In her illuminating book,

---

[1] Yuval Noah Harari, *Sapiens: A Brief History of Humankind* (London: Vintage, 2011).

[2] I agree with Jonathan Culler when he lists 'thick description over simplifying principle' (*The Literary in Theory*, 30) as one of the distinguishing attributes of literature. But I argue that it is much more than that. By 'thick description', Culler largely means what one would call detailed, complex, multi-faceted, even at times contradictory, descriptions.

[3] Anna Lowenhaupt Tsing, *The Mushroom at the End of the World: On the Possibility of Life in Capitalist Ruins* (Princeton and Oxford: Princeton University Press, 2015), 37; italics in original.

Literature Against Fundamentalism. Tabish Khair, Oxford University Press. © Tabish Khair (2024).
DOI: 10.1093/oso/9780198919582.003.0002

she offers a number of such stories, often those of immigrants and war veterans gathering matsutake, the most valuable mushroom in the world, in different countries. She knits them together to suggest, as the subtitle of her book puts it, 'the possibility of life in capitalist ruins', which also includes an alternative critique of capitalism.

Tsing is writing long after what can be called 'postcolonial' anthropology has come to be established and accepted in her discipline. This is anthropology that listens to the stories of others. It grew as a critique of the dominant colonial tradition of anthropological writing, which was just as dependent on stories, but mostly those of the colonial or European 'self'. A quintessential example of this colonial tradition is offered in the writings of Henry Morton Stanley—of 'Dr Livingstone, I presume' fame—and Sven Lindqvist, the Swedish writer and historian, has succinctly excavated Stanley's narratives to reveal the remains of all the other stories that they hide, evade, obscure, even erase.[4] The necessary criticism of the colonial monopoly of the European self telling stories about others has led to the practice of anthropologists listening to the stories that others have to tell. Its development can also be traced in related fields, such as Subaltern studies. The best anthropologists today, such as Tsing, can raise this to the level of theory and method.

And yet, from the perspective of literature, they are faced with the same problem that eventually made us question the stories of people like Stanley: no story or narrative can be accepted on face value. Even a single word cannot be taken for granted across two people, as Chekhov knew. Just as there is no guarantee that Stanley is telling the truth, there is no guarantee of truth in the words of a Vietnamese immigrant or a US war veteran. The matter is more complex in at least two different but at times overlapping ways: (a) there is no guarantee that the truth of the narrator is the truth as it was out there, while there is often also no way of ascertaining the truth out there; and (b) there is no guarantee that the language of the narrator is the same as the language of the reader, even when they share the same language.

[4] Sven Lindqvist, *'Exterminate All the Brutes': One Man's Odyssey into the Heart of Darkness and the Origins of European Genocide*, first published 1197, trans. Joan Tate (London: Granta, 2002).

Literature cannot be conflated with 'storytelling'. Storytelling is related to the definition of language. While I agree with Harari that Homo Sapiens is (primarily) a storytelling animal that thinks in stories rather than numbers or graphs, I particularly stress this to be understood as based on a prior argument for the distinctiveness of human language, defined as an abstract system of differential signs. True, scholars have convincingly argued that other animals and birds interpret their surroundings and create their own 'experiential worlds', as Amitav Ghosh puts it.[5] He notes, 'Any pet owner knows that a dog understands as meaningful the relationship between the home, the park, and certain times of day. For the dog, is this a "chronology" or a "narrative"?'[6] Thinking of this as a kind of storytelling, Ghosh quotes the anthropologist Thom van Dooren's claim that 'experiencing beings like Penguins' also 'inhabit an endlessly storied world'.[7] However, to turn the complex experiencing and inhabiting of the world that animals are no doubt capable of into a 'story', as understood by human beings, seems to betray the same kind of unsubstantiated generalizations—if one leaves aside the matter of anthropomorphism—that the confusion between the language of bees or trees *and* a language like Latin or Hindi would. To turn stories into a being's memoried relationship to places etc. is also to turn them from fiction to fact, and turn language from an abstract system of largely arbitrary signs to perhaps a direct system of symbols. One simple indication of this resides in the realization that we do not just tell stories about what exists or existed but also about what never existed and might never exist (as Harari notes). We tell stories or write poems not just about what we know or see but also what we have never known or seen or can possibly know or see. God and related matters are an obvious example. This complex activity is largely enabled by the fact that the language of human beings is a very different construct than the language of birds or bees though I am fully willing to concede that the difference would inevitably contain not just advantages but also disadvantages, not just something gained but also possibly something lost.

[5] Amitav Ghosh, *The Nutmeg's Curse: Parables of a Planet in Crisis* (London and Gurugram: Allen Lane, Penguin Random House, 2021), 202

[6] Ghosh, *ibid.*, 202.

[7] Ghosh, *ibid.*, 203.

One can argue that, at least in some cases, the truth of a narrator's 'story' can be independently verified. For instance, if one person claims that a genocide did not take place in a village and another claims that it did, it might be possible (though, in real life, it is often very difficult) to objectively verify which claim is true. But even this solution, which is seldom possible in any case, given the 'variables' involved, is not a real solution. Because it reduces stories to something else: an event, a happening, etc. What is proved or disproved is this event. The tendency to confirm a story—or any statement in a language—with reference to something outside it, is essentially the same as the insistence of the religious on a fundamentalist reading of their texts. It posits a 'God' whose prior existence smoothens out, justifies, and validates the text. However, the agnostic reading that literature demands, and teaches, takes place within the text, without ignoring its contexts. It is this that one fails to teach their students if literature is taught *only* as entertainment, politics, social realism, linguistic play etc. Not only is there no 'fake news' inside literature, no matter how fanciful its narrative, the reading of literature as literature is the best way to learn to decipher the cries and accusations of 'fake news' in the world.

Literature teaches us to tell the truth in language, in text and context, and not with reference to an outside power, whether God, event or fact. The 'story' itself—as a version of 'reality' and 'language'—cannot be reduced to an event, which can or cannot be verified. One needs to approach the story as a story, with the 'agnosticism' that I am talking about: the agnosticism of language when read as literature. The agnosticism of literature is not a matter of ambivalence, if 'ambivalence' is used in the sense of sitting comfortably on the fence. It is a much more disturbing matter. Plato saw this clearly, and therefore banished the poet. As theorists like Martha Nussbaum have noted, literature calls upon the reader to make judgements. However, these judgements—without which the reader can make sense of neither the language nor the story (including obvious elements like character) of literature, or, for the matter, their complex interrelationship, is not the same as a court judgement.[8] It is a judgement that has to be made in every instance of the reading, and is complete in that instance, but

---

[8] Martha Nussbaum makes similar points in her book, *Poetic Justice: The Literary Imagination and Public Life* (Boston: Beacon, 1995). She also illustrates that reading literature

that calls upon to be made—and sometimes unmade—time and again as the reading proceeds. It is a judgement that often stands firmly on one side, for instance that of the 'hero', without condemning the other side, for instance the villain, to the electric chair, as many conventional judges would. 'The techniques of literary narrative in particular work to constitute readers as observers who sympathise but who must in the end judge.'[9] Unlike what Plato thought, the sympathy, empathy, contradiction, complexity, polyvocality etc. which literature makes part of this activity of judging leads not to confused or lesser or 'false' judgements, but to more complete ones. Finding the 'truth' becomes an activity: it is placed in living context, and is not handed down—as, for instance, is the case with fundamentalist and even many religious interpretations of God's judgements—fixed and readymade forever. The position adopted is, once again, that of an agnostic: it rests on the assumption that one has to both trust and distrust, believe and not believe, empathize and judge, and one has to come to a contextualized conclusion through such a process of reading. This marks not the relief of lack of judging that is attributed to ('entertaining') literature by those who read superficially or distractedly, but a far more complex, self-aware, relational, and endless process of judgement—one that highlights the etymological residue to both 'the capacity to make a decision' and 'discernment' that also adheres to 'judgement', sometimes implicitly questioning its currently dominant and more hasty sense of an 'authoritative verdict' or the 'imposition of a penalty'.

Like God, this agnosticism of literature is not a question of existence or non-existence, proof or lack of proof. Both positions, as I illustrate further in this book, do not solve the problem of God. Neither do they explain literature. Language has to be taken into account along with its mutually defining relationship to everything outside it. To understand this, one has to state two obvious facts. First, literature is written in language. Second, literature is not just about language. In other words, literature is written in language about that which cannot and will not be confined to language. So-called literary language,

creates a model for judging that some actual judges apply—she calls them 'the literary judge'—and others do not, and this is a good example of what I dub the agnostic reading that literature demands and its effects.

[9] Jonathan Culler, *The Literary in Theory* (Stanford: Stanford University, Press, 2007), 31.

in particular, refuses to delimit its meanings and concerns, as 'scientific' or 'business' or 'administrative' language does (or pretends to do). Hence, literature qua literature is where the problems, possibilities, and limits of language can no longer be avoided. These problems are also the problems of philosophy and religion, when they are not nailed down by rituals and fundamentalist readings: problems of reality and representation, at its simplest and most complex.

This perspective allows one not only to accept the validity of mimetic or expressivist definitions of literature, but even allows space for journalists who celebrate a text because it is 'controversial' or 'radical' and academics who study a text because it contains words of hoary etymological significance or fresh Creole/dialectical provenance. One can understand why a new language use or a disturbing social issue employed by a literary text can and should be read as a point in its favour, for the text is bringing into language what could not be contained within that language, or not until then.

Some of what I am discussing has to do with literary technique, a fact known to writers and scholars for millennia. Let us take the ancient Sanskrit aesthetic theory of *nayika*s or heroines, which, when paraphrased, seems quite simple: a theorized version of what, in English, would be called character types. Consider this example of a type of nayika taken from Vishwanatha Kaviraja's fourteenth-century *Sahityadarpana* (The Mirror of Literature): the lovesick woman or nayika, or, in Anglophone terms, the female character type whose husband has gone abroad:

> The dress is one you've worn before,
> And the bracelet on your wrist
> And the jewelled belt you carry on your hips,
> So why does it all seem too big,
> Dear friend, on this lovely spring day
> That buzzing bees make lovelier?[10]

As is obvious, what is being 'described' has not been said but suggested. To say this in 'transparent' language—one that presumes unfailing 'communication'—would be to turn it into something other

---

[10] Pollock's translation, quoted from Audrey Truschke, *Culture of Encounters: Sanskrit at the Mughal Court* (New York: Columbia University Press, 2016), 159.

than literature. In effect this: despite the fact that it is spring, a season associated with love, as the bees indicate, it appears that you have lost some weight, as your usual dress is hanging loose on your body. In the poem, the suffering of the nayika is felt with greater impact because it is not defined in words and it is left to the reader to flesh out in her imagination. Of course, the reader is not abandoned in a forest of haphazard words. Various signposts are there, ranging from the looseness of the attire, which suggests loss of weight, to the spring day with buzzing bees, which suggests life, sex, and love. The supposedly 'suggestive' nature of literature arises from literature's ability to both address and say something beyond language, as this simple example illustrates.

It is important to pause here and note that I am not arguing that the language of literature is different—more heightened, ambiguous etc.—than ordinary language. I totally agree with Stanley Fish when he notes, and I will quote him extensively, that

> I challenge the opposition between a basic or neutral language that is responsible to or reflects the world of objective fact and a language that reflects the uniqueness of individual or subjective perception. This distinction in turn is attached to another, between language we ordinarily use in managing the business of everyday life and the language of literature, and as a result 'ordinary life' is detached from the realm of perspective and values (now the province of subjectivity and literature) and turned into a purely formal structure that exists apart from any particular purpose or situation. My strategy [...] is to rescue ordinary language from this impoverishing characterization by arguing that at its heart is precisely the realm of values, intentions, and purposes which is often assumed to be the exclusive property of literature.[11]

The point I am making, and I return to it again and again, is that literature enables—demands—that we work with the problem of language, which is the problem of the mutually constitutive relationships between language and reality, instead of ignoring or, in disciplinary

[11] Stanley Fish, *Is There A Text in This Classroom?* (Harvard: Harvard University Press, 1982), 10.

fields, constraining and attempting to erase them. Fundamentalism is at the opposite end of the spectrum to this approach.

Hence, I argue that the social, political, and linguistic impacts of a literary text are only the most visible and perhaps simplest of its literary virtues. Even 'literary technique' or 'aesthetics' is, from my perspective, either a misnomer or just a superficial description. The best of literature always presses against the limits of language at least in its socio-historical context. Language, any language, allows one to say some things and prevents one from saying some other things. Sometimes what is said is a matter of historicity: some discourses can be made in a certain historical and cultural context, and some others cannot. For instance, in nineteenth-century Europe, it was easier to talk of various races and miscegenation than of a 'mixed marriage'; homosexuality could be conceptualized in terms of 'sodomy', as Marcel Proust does, rather than 'gay rights'. This, of course, is not simply a matter of progress: for instance, there have been historical periods when things which are desired but seem impossible today would have appeared quite normal. But while some of the limits of language are socio-historically determined and might be crossed in time and space—hence, perhaps reducing the literary value of a literary text— some other limits seem to be built into the natures of some languages and, more generally, the relationship of language to the world outside language.

What I am stating here by focussing on the 'material' of literature— language—can also be discussed using other concepts, such as the relationship between objectivity and reality, or the dualism of the brain and the mind. But there is no need to get into those complications, which often leave us lost in cunning passages and contrived corridors. Actually, in a different book, I might have argued that the very notion of objectivity is flawed when we talk of it as exhausting reality: it is not that objectivity is the only thing that exists in reality, as many assume. Instead, objectivity is the only thing that allows us to equally ('rationally') discuss whatever reality might be. I have made a similar point about reason too, as the two are related points. The achievements of the sciences and the 'scientific' social sciences have been enabled by their stress on objectivity not because it exhausted reality, but because it enabled an equal and reasoned discussion. We have always known that reality for human beings, partly or largely or maybe even entirely because of language, can never be studied in a solely objective fashion—so much from our feelings, dreams, and beliefs to our social interactions and rituals have a large subjective surcharge. However, it can only be *discussed* in an objective manner—or with the use of 'reason'—instead of personal, communal, and other revelations.[12]

Puhpowee and Emily Brontë

Let me illustrate the above observations with reference to a recent discussion in a book that I consider literature, for the reasons given here: it uses language successfully to talk of what cannot be reduced to language. As stated elsewhere too, in my book I have concentrated on known classics and on books of narrative fiction, for the sake of convenience, largely leaving out non-fiction prose and poetry, as they would have demanded longer exegesis and more terminology. However, the book I refer to here is 'non-fiction prose', and it often aspires to poetry: Robert Macfarlane's *Underland*.[13]

Macfarlane talks about two matters that elude language, particularly the language of transparency (and visibility): deep time and all that lies beneath our feet. This is not an easy feat. How can one talk of time that does not seem to move, especially in our age of jumping,

---

[12] True, reason does not exhaust all modes of human experience. There is growing evidence that what we call 'reason' is only one of the ways in which human beings experience and think, as, among others, Martha Nussbaum suggests. Does that mean that one can dispense with reason? No, and definitely not in science. *Science depends on reason not because reason exhausts human experience or knowledge, but because it enables an equal and negotiable **exchange** of human experience and knowledge.* In this, the assumptions of science differ from those of religion. Science, working with reason, depends on the fact that any two human beings can discuss and debate its findings at the same level of language and experience. 'Reason' can be employed to show that one is right and the other wrong. In religion, which is based on subjective experience, this is not possible. One of the two versions has to be accepted (which is usually the case), or both, despite their contradictions (which happens less often). That is why religion requires gurus, revelations, and prophets, while science calls for repeatable experiments. With religion, one has to choose to accept (or reject) a subjective experience: the reported miracle, the personal vision, the revealed text, the wise teacher, etc. To call for the miracle to be repeated or the angel to return with a revelation under, shall we say, laboratory conditions (or within a format of shared and equal reason) is to miss the point of faith, as Søren Kierkegaard, among others, has highlighted.

[13] Robert Macfarlane, *Underland: A Deep Time Journey*, first published 2019 (London: Penguin Random House, 2020).

frolicking, running time? And how can one talk of that which cannot be seen—because it lies under us—and that can mostly be accessed only at the risk of changing it (for instance, by digging into the earth)? But Macfarlane makes it even more difficult for himself: he chooses to write about it not as fiction, which would have allowed him greater leeway, but as non-fiction. *Underland* won the Stanford Dolman Travel Book Award in 2020, and is slotted under the 'non-fiction' category. This generic tagging is necessary and accurate—and, inevitably, misleading. For instance, apart from the poetry of the descriptions in between, each of the three parts of the book is preceded by a short 'chamber', which is almost entirely generically alien to non-fiction prose, combining elements that, if unleashed on the unwary reader, will be classified as poetry. Obviously, Macfarlane is pressing language to the utmost in his bid to talk about what is not and cannot ever be transparent and visible through language.

However, I will not look at this large endeavour in this admirable book. Instead, I will look at a short section in which Macfarlane overtly discusses the attempt to expand language so as to enable it to contain more than it does. These are three pages in the chapter titled 'The Understorey' in Part I: Seeing (Britain), and they are spliced into the narration of a long walk that the author took in the Epping Forest in the north-east of London with the biologist, Merlin Sheldrake. It succeeds a section in which Sheldrake notes—something that I have felt for decades now and have, to some extent, studied (for it can be studied)—how our dominant conceptions of existence, evolution, science, nature, etc., are shaped by the 'language of . . . free-marketry'. However, he also expresses dissatisfaction with the (in my view, minority and institutionally marginalized) 'socialist version'.[14]

They are essentially talking of fungi, especially mycorrhizae, which have recently been discovered as providing networks of sustenance between trees, including those of different species, while themselves living in a symbiotic relationship with the trees. When Sheldrake expresses dissatisfaction with the language in which such discussions are carried out—those of dominant capitalism and opposing socialism—Macfarlane notes that 'perhaps we need an entirely new language system to talk about fungi . . . We need to speak in spores'. Sheldrake

[14] Ibid.

strongly agrees and adds: 'That's the job of writers and artists and poets and all the rest of you.'[15]

It is then that the three-page interlude about language that I mentioned earlier crops up. It starts with reference to the work of Robin Wall Kimmerer. A botanist and the author, among other texts, of *Gathering Moss: A Natural and Cultural History of Mosses* (2021), Kimmerer is also a member of the Citizen Potawatomi Nation; it is a word from the Native American language, Potawatomi, that initiates the discussion. Macfarlane quotes Kimmerer on the Potawatomi word *puhpowee*, 'which might be translated as "the force which causes mushrooms to push up from the earth overnight"' and that, despite all its terminologies, 'Western science has no such term, no words to hold this mystery'.[16] Macfarlane correctly notes that this 'missing something is predominantly the acknowledgement of life in the more-than-human world, an indifference which is grained into language not just at the level of individual words, but as the deeper-down levels of grammar and syntax'.[17]

If one transposes this discussion, using Sheldrake's challenge to poets and artists as the springing board, into the matrix of my discussion in this book, one immediately has access to prominent aspects of literature. One of them contains elements like Pound's invocation to 'make it new' and Orwell's practical prescriptions to keep language fresh in his essay, 'Politics and the English Language' (1946). This would mean a constant challenging and renewing of vocabulary, syntax, grammar as they exist in any language: something that, in different ways, much of literature does. Another aspect would include the grasping of other words—even the creation of new words, either from slang, dialect, etc., or from other languages. In some ways, Macfarlane and Kimmerer have made this possible by putting 'puhpowee' on record, and it will just take, say, a good poem to remove the scare quotes around that alien word and insert it into the English language.

This, as Sheldrake notes, is something that literature can—and should—do. It is an aspect of what I mean when I say that literature is a thinking device. Macfarlane continues this train of thought and

---

[15] Ibid., 111.
[16] Ibid.
[17] Ibid.

hopes, with Kimmerer, for a 'grammar of animacy', for instance.[18] Kimmerer notes that projects have 'recently been started around the world to gain even the most basic vocabularies for the experiences of life and death in the Anthropocene'. But she also records that such 'stuttering attempts to speak' have 'generated ugly new terms for an ugly epoch: "geotraumatics", "planetary dysphoria", "apex-guilt"'.[19] These necessary terms, Macfarlane observes, 'stick in the throat in two ways: they are difficult to utter and hard to swallow', and he concedes that only one of these new terms ('species loneliness') resonates with him.[20]

Macfarlane does not take this further. He leaves the discussion poised on the verge of the possibility of a new language to address an obscure/d aspect of existence. But I cannot help noticing the limitations of this hope, especially as even Macfarlane, a writer who can use words creatively—make them new, in Pound's words—finds these necessary terms 'difficult to utter and hard to swallow'. Within the circumference of my call for literature, this is not just a matter of creating a new language; it is also a matter of the relationship between language and reality. Though the need to keep language alive and to make it anew is an aspect of literature, there is also another side of it: the awareness that language is not enough, will never be enough, and is especially limited when confined solely to the role of transparency and communication and visibility. Like the underland explored by Macfarlane, much of reality will remain difficult to see and/or it will shift shapes when accessed. Language pinned down to the disciplinary requirement—necessary, I say again and again, in its academic contexts—of transparency is always language that, now or sometime, becomes difficult to utter and hard to swallow.

Sheldrake is absolutely right when he calls on writers to create a new language—but this language will never be just a language. This language is literature—language that is instinctively aware of its necessity and limits. This language, as I keep noting, demands the agnostic reading of literature. In this book, I argue that this is what distinguishes literature: its very use of language, because it does not treat

---

[18] Ibid., 112.
[19] Ibid., 113.
[20] Ibid.

language as transparent, smooth, sufficient, and, despite how popular critics read much of current fiction, representative. However, its meanings are not relative but contextual, and being contextual they are also—as is the case with the other, for the other always presents its face to the self—precarious. One example, out of many, that comes to mind immediately is from the beginning of a novel I greatly admire, and about which I have written extensively in the past, Emily Brontë's *Wuthering Heights*.

Lockwood's first-person narrative in *Wuthering Heights* begins with a date—1801—that locates the text not only temporally, but also generically: the text is a diary or some associated genre. Rooted in a Latin word with the later meaning of 'daily journal', itself derived from the earlier meaning of 'daily allowance', a diary contains discrete entries, usually arranged by date, of what happened to the diarist over a period of days. Originally written by hand, which one can safely assume is how both Emily Brontë and Lockwood would have envisioned the text in the first half of the nineteenth century, a diary is both intimate and immediate: it contains opinions and feeling based on the direct observation of the diarist.

This is exactly how *Wuthering Heights* seems to start. Soon after, the novel deviates widely (and purposefully) from the generic requirements of the diary: most obviously, it consists of a report, largely by Nelly, of what happened in the past, and has little to do with the diarist or their present. But the first few paragraphs stay true to the reader's expectations from the genre:

> 1801.—I have just returned from a visit to my landlord—the solitary neighbour that I shall be troubled with. This is certainly a beautiful country! In all England, I do not believe that I could have fixed on a situation so completely removed from the stir of society. A perfect misanthropist's heaven—and Mr. Heathcliff and I are such a suitable pair to divide the desolation between us.[21]

Jane Austen is rightly celebrated as a magnificent practitioner of literary irony, the opening line from *Pride and Prejudice* being often quoted

---

[21] Emile Brontë, *Wuthering Heights*, first published 1847, ed. A. Lewis (New York: W. W. Norton and Company, 2019), 3.

as an example: irony being based, in all its forms, on the gap between what is said and what is left unsaid, and between text and context. But if that line is the perfect example of verbal irony, then the first paragraph of *Wuthering Heights* is a brilliant example of a specimen of structural irony. If structural irony is characterized by the author introducing a 'structural feature that serves to sustain a duplex meaning and evaluation throughout the work', then Lockwood, as a particular kind of limited first-person narrator, is that structural feature.[22] This is not immediately obvious, and hence the irony of the situation—and even the language—is lost on a virgin reader of the novel. But one cannot return to the novel and fail to note the deep irony of the lines quoted earlier, in which Lockwood gets everything *wrong* about the people and the place.

Brontë warns soon enough, in the next four or five pages that follow: Lockwood gets almost everything wrong about what he witnesses in and around the house, including the relationships of the people to each other and to the house. Returning from there to the first few lines of his diary—and with greater force once we have gotten to learn more about Heathcliff—one notices that Lockwood's reading of both his landlord and the country are mistaken. Lockwood sees Heathcliff as a version of himself: an urbane man who likes solitude. The urbane and largely urban nature of Lockwood's 'misanthropy' is revealed by his desire to link himself to Heathcliff in their very solitude: 'solitary neighbour', 'a suitable pair to divide the desolation between us'. This, it is soon discovered, is very different from what Mr Heathcliff is. While the 'nature' of Mr Heathcliff is questioned throughout the novel by some characters and continues to (needlessly to my mind) bother many critics, it is indubitable by the end of the novel that Heathcliff, unlike Lockwood, does not decide to 'remove' himself from the 'stir of society'. For Lockwood it is a choice, for Heathcliff it is compulsion. Lockwood gets, so to say, tired of company and takes an occasional break in nature; Heathcliff does not care for people, not even, his own son. And, strangely, while Lockwood is afraid of committing himself deeply to others and falling in love, as the only vignette from his immediate past reveals, Heathcliff has so deeply committed himself to

[22] M. H. Abrams and G. G. Harpham, *A Glossary of Literary Terms* (Stamford, CT: Cengage Learning, 2015), 185.

Catherine that he can neither forget nor forgive, neither live freely himself nor let others live freely.

No two solitary people can be more different in their solitariness than Lockwood and Heathcliff. What 'solitary' means to Lockwood does not apply to Heathcliff. But if Lockwood gets Heathcliff entirely wrong, he gets the 'country' around Wuthering Heights, buffeted by winds at a higher level than the village and Thrushcross Grange further down, surrounded by the desolate moors, entirely wrong too. The storm that maroons Lockwood in Wuthering Heights—prompting Heathcliff to warn him to 'make no more rash journeys on these hills'—proves that the description, 'beautiful country', is not appropriate so far from Thrushcross Grange. Nature around Wuthering Heights is not beautiful; it is closer to 'sublime' in the Burkean sense: it evokes astonishment and contains a hint of horror. This is not the 'bliss of solitude' of Wordsworthian daffodils, surely growing in abundance in the park surrounding Thrushcross Grange in the right season; this is more a matter of the dark ecology that Timothy Morton talks about.

What do we make of a novel whose very first lines are meant to do two things: (a) contest the meanings attributed to words, places, and people by the narrator, and (b) make this deeply ironic contestation fully visible only in retrospect, often during a second reading of the novel? What is being narrated even in the initial pages is full of holes, gaps, silences, misunderstandings, none of which is transparently stated in language, and some of which actually makes sense only after the entire novel has been read and digested. This small matter of gaps and silences in the initial pages is integral to the larger structure of the novel. The meaning and significances of this great novel are contextual, though only accessible through a close attention to what the text says and does not say, what it shows and hides.

The double or circular structure of the novel has often been remarked by critics, but usually this is read as a relationship between the doubles or the two halves of the circle: how the Cathy–Hareton segment completes, redeems, annotates, or accommodates the Catherine–Heathcliff segment. I want to make the associated but different argument that the structure is not just a bid to make meanings clear as we read on, but an attempt to make us return and discover new meanings in what has already been perused. It is intended to make us notice the gaps and silences, to read not just the text behind the visible context, as we did the first time round, but the hidden context behind the text this time round. At the heart of this novel is not just a contestation of meanings, but an engagement with the precarity and significance of meanings. The uncertainty of what the relationships that Lockwood observes in the first few pages mean (or, even, are), the shift in the significance of 'beautiful' nature, the 'cats' in a chair that are actually dead rabbits, etc.: all these small insufficiencies and errors of meaning lead, early on, by way of the difficult-to-decipher inscriptions in Catherine's book, to the two nightmares whose meanings critics have since been deciphering. All of *Wuthering Heights* is a narrative where much of the story has to be excavated by the reader, and this excavation calls for not just reading but contemplation. Above all, this excavation helps us access the precarity of meanings and significances that the given language—in this case that of the well-meaning but limited and conservative Nelly much of the time—seems to fail to cover: the entire story of Heathcliff is a story of such precarity, but he is by no means alone in this novel where almost all significant characters wrestle to some extent against the precarity of meanings and significance in a world which is always, as a rule, narrated differently from the way they experience it.

2

Literature, Gaps, and Historicity

We are all, as Jonathan Culler rightly notes, 'ineluctably in theory'.[1]
My refusal to examine literature by taking recourse to the language of
some theory or the other is *not* based on a dismissal of theory, which
evidently has its uses, but on my understanding, as explicated in this
book, of a *definitive* aspect of literature[2]: literature is not just about
what can be communicated in language, but also what cannot be,
now and/or for ever. Hence, it demands an engagement with both
language and what is not language: such as gaps, silences, noise, etc.
between the words and in the words. It seems to me to be a mistake
to reduce literature to language, when literature, by definition, differs
from other disciplines in its conscious and artful attempt to narrate
both within and without language. Literary theory, in that sense, is
always to be used with full knowledge of its essential *limitation in dealing with literature* as and in language. Moreover, while literary theory is
essential for a reading of literature at a disciplinary, academic level, I
have avoided its discourse also because, as argued in this book, literature is the oldest and most common 'thinking device' partly because
it engages with 'life' or 'reality' in all kinds of spoken, written, and
essentially non-specialized language. To talk about it in the highly specialized, disciplinary language of theory is to perform two activities
alien to its nature: reduce what it *does not and cannot* put in language to
a kind of meta-language, and remove its import as a 'thinking device'
available in ordinary, non-specialized language to all who can listen
and read (and turn it instead into a highly specialized, ordained, and
disciplinary cogitative activity for a select priesthood).

[1] Jonathan Culler, *The Literary in Theory*, 3.
[2] What this means is that *all works in language* that demand to be heard/read within
language and outside it, with gaps, silences, noise etc. not evaded or explained away,
are essentially literature.

Literature Against Fundamentalism. Tabish Khair, Oxford University Press. © Tabish Khair (2024).
DOI: 10.1093/oso/9780198919582.003.0003

Of course, *there was never a time when we were not in theory*—though the mediation of theory, in a way that parallels the development of money into capital, was considered secondary to what it was mediating. Liberal humanism was itself a theory (or a collocation of linked theories) that often considered its mediation natural and transparent and hence could pretend to be non-theoretical. In due course, the supposed failures of liberal humanism were obvious, not least because some of its assumptions left the historical humanity of people like me out of pur/view. Liberal humanism, with its roots in European Enlightenment, accepted non-Europeans, but always under the threat of potential erasure as non-European. This universality of 'Man' naturally translated into the universality of 'Literature': good literature was of universal relevance and of timeless significance. It was this, above all, that later twentieth-century literary theory set out to combat. As Peter Barry paraphrases liberal humanist perspectives on literature, if 'good literature was of timeless relevance' and 'transcend[ed] the limitations and peculiarities of the age it was written in', then, logically speaking, 'the literary text contain[ed] its own meaning within itself' and in order to understand it we had to detach the text from its 'contexts' and study it 'in isolation'.[3]

As against these tenets of liberal humanism, Barry notes that twentieth-century literary theory stressed 'five points': 'Politics is pervasive, language is constitutive, truth is provisional, meaning is contingent, human nature is a myth'.[4] In essence, literary and cultural 'theory'—despite its increasing abstraction—was a bid to return to fragmented historicity: the 'universal' essentially refracted into endless particulars. This was not History, as it had been in the past, for there could be no single narrative uniting its historical particulars in any given direction. Thus, the return to historicity by 'theory' also marked the end of History in some accounts.

In fact, in the cultural fields, the most acute dismissal of universality etc. probably took some form of postmodernism. Even if one sees postmodernism as a kind of late modernism, as some critics do, it has to be noted that while modernism to a large extent *mourned* the fragments

[3] Peter Barry, *Beginning Theory: An Introduction to Literary and Cultural Theory*, first published 1995 (Manchester and New York: Manchester University Press, 2009), 17.
[4] Ibid., 35.

that T. S. Eliot shores up in his poems, postmodernism not only internalized the fragmentation—prompting Ihab Hassan's distinction between modernist paranoia and postmodernist schizophrenia—it also *celebrated* it, at least in its inevitability. The dominantly elegiac tone that marks Eliot's modernist 'The Love Song of J. Alfred Prufrock' would find no or little place in a postmodernist story like Thomas Pynchon's 'Entropy', despite the obvious fragmentation of 'life' in both.

Today, as I write at the cusp of the second and third decade of the twenty-first century, some of these postmodernist insights evoke less enthusiasm than they did three decades ago. Like Eliot, the great modernist, the last few decades have seen many grasp at religion for stability. Sometimes this has overlapped with or translated into fundamentalist ideologies. The end of History, even in Francis Fukuyama's optimistic version, has also led to the rise of combating iterations of brutality.[5] The Covid pandemic, which is when I wrote some of this book, further complicated matters—not, alas, clarified them, as was to be hoped. If no one Truth prevails, then, unfortunately, there is also the phenomenon of 'fake news' and post-truth.[6]

We tend to forget that all 'truths' are contextual (but not necessarily relative), even in the supposedly 'universal' sciences: 'Nor does "absolutely true" mean true independently of any context. We can only judge the world from within some kind of framework'.[7] Any statement, any 'fact' can only be true in a certain context, and it is likely to change when the context changes. The truth of sub-atomic particles exists in that context, and the truth of planetary systems in our universe exists in that context. These are not exclusive, but it would be a seriously confused scientist who would expect the rules and conditions that obtain within an atom to be exactly the same as the rules and conditions that obtain in our planetary system made up of those very atoms. This is what I mean by contextual. Relativism, on the other hand, or at least extreme relativism, extracts the observer from the context and makes the observer's version paramount. Here the observer becomes the

---

[5] Francis Fukuyama, *The End of History and the Last Man* (New York: Free Press, 1992).

[6] Johan Farkas and Jannick Schou, *Post-Truth, Fake News and Democracy: Mapping the Politics of Falsehood* (London and New York: Routledge, 2019).

[7] Terry Eagleton, *After Theory* (London: Penguin Books, 2004), 107.

truth, as if their observation is beyond any context, as if the observer has no context.

Truth and, by definition, thought are not to be confused with the recycling of sacred or fixed ideas. Thought is not to be confused with outrage or opinions or feelings, though each of these might play a role in thinking to an extent. There is nothing universal about thought, if by universal it is meant, as the liberal humanists allegedly did, 'unchanging and fixed'. Byung-Chul Han correctly notes in an array of texts that the medium of thinking is quiet, now perhaps being destroyed by digital communication.[8] The quantitative advantages of computation do not apply to matters like thinking about joy, happiness, suffering, pain, loss, fear, etc., and, as Han notes further, '[f]ulfilment and meaning cannot be explained on quantitative grounds'.[9]

It is this thinking about 'joy, happiness, suffering, pain, loss, fear, etc'. that happens in literature, and it happens in ways that are decidedly not quantitative—not even in terms of the language used. Words are required, words are inevitable, but they are not considered sufficient. On the other hand, there is nothing that they can be replaced with— no 'revelation', for instance, that so easily helps the religious (and, as we shall see, helped Job) skirt unanswered or unanswerable questions. In literature, one is faced with the starkness of the language of the text,

[8] There is an argument, which needs to be explored in greater detail, that digitalized communication makes it easier to evade difference, and to stereotype and ridicule it. In other words, it is easier to avoid facing the other on computers, iPad, etc. At its simplest, this can be explained with reference to an ordinary conversation: in a conversation one faces the other, and this face-to-face interaction often modulates both the positions. Arguments that refuse to acknowledge this lead to a fight, which ends the conversation. In political terms, this can be seen as the difference between a stiffly fought democratic election and civil war. Politics depends on conversations, which include but also absorb arguments. These can be called debates, if by debate one means a continued discussion, a critical conversation. When argument leads to a total fracture and ends the conversation, one moves from politics to war. There is enough empirical evidence that a face-to-face interaction often makes even obdurate opponents modulate their statements and, in the better cases, their views. This does not happen in computerized interactions where, for instance, one simply 'unfriends' a person one disagrees with, and algorithms surround one with those who share the same prejudices. Hence, while cyberspace seems to crawl with differences, it does not necessarily enable a better engagement with difference.
[9] Byung-Chul Han, *The Scent of Time*, first published 2009, trans. Daniel Steuer (Cambridge and Medford: Polity, 2017), 34.

and the knowledge that writer, readers, contexts—in other words, a million shades of 'historicity'—are both shaping that language, in its writing and reading, and being shaped by that language.

Literature was never what was universally and eternally the same; literature was what could be read fruitfully in different ways in different spaces.[10] As almost all living scholars would agree today, Shakespeare is not universal and eternal in the sense that we still read Shakespeare as he was read in the seventeenth or the nineteenth century. Sameness is not what makes Shakespeare 'universal' or 'eternal'; it is the relevance of difference, as I try to illustrate with an 'ahistorical' reading of *Hamlet* later in this book.[11] Shakespeare's appeal to each generation—and perhaps each culture—has changed and continues to alter. He is 'universal' only to the extent that his texts are capable of ever-changing readings without loss of depth and meanings. They enable a conversation. The reason this happens is that his texts gain from what I call the process of reading (a form of deep attention); they allow space for the reader to dive into them. Not all plays or sonnets from Shakespeare's age do so, or not as much.

What if, as I have suggested, it is not sameness, but difference that is the definition of universality and timeless significance? There is a kind of precarious universality, as is inevitable because in literature not only the contexts (author–reader, at its simplest) change, even the texts change (as we shall see when we look at Twain's novel below) and their relationships change: this is also a matter of the book, or the written text, as we shall see in a later chapter. All this requires us to engage with the difference of a text written in a different time by a different person for different reasons—and to engage with it in the context of our time, for we can never stand out of context. Yes, literature is not above history. In the human experience, nothing is. Our very words come

---

[10] This space is not to be confused with pace. One can argue that screen reading is far too fast: for instance (as stated), your eyes move down the page, but the cursor moves the line in the opposite direction too. So that you can read faster, and faster. To read fast is a bit like driving fast: you get to your destination sooner, but you see much less on the way. Literature has never been only about getting to your destination.

[11] In theoretical terms, my reading of *Hamlet* can be aligned with 'presentism', just as the reading of *Huckleberry Finn* that follows in this chapter can be aligned to the various schools associated with 'historicism': I have avoided such theoretical terminology, but obviously, as was the case of the blind men of Hindoostan, literature is the elephant that allows and demands all such modes of address.

to us trailing the mud of various histories, always multiple, sometimes contradictory. Nothing Plato could do about that, and neither can we. It is, therefore, not surprising that historical readings of literature predominate—I include aesthetic readings, sometimes reactionary in their loud ahistoricity, among these readings, as I do social, political, Darwinist, and other readings. By historical, I mean a reading of literature that looks at everything else around it. This is absolutely necessary. And, as I argue in this book, this is also *not* sufficient.

Why is it not sufficient?

Take, for instance, a *problematic word* in a purely historical text. Say, the word 'nigger' in racist texts from the nineteenth century. It is easy and necessary to condemn and excise such a word, and this is a simple matter as long as the text is *not* a work of literature. However, in a work of literature, this matter gets much more complex. I illustrate this with an example: reading the N-word in *Huckleberry Finn* in the historical context, by illustrating what the novel, as literature, says even when it seems to use words of a doubtful provenance. I argue that, in effect, the novel exceeds the historical circumstances of its inscription, while its language remains inescapably mired in that history.

L-words in *Huckleberry Finn*

The most commonly recurring controversy in American literature centres around the use of the N-word, and sooner or later it tends to involve Mark Twain's *Adventures of Huckleberry Finn*. There are essentially four positions on the use of this word in the novel, of which only three need to be addressed, because the fourth position is that of a racist and has no intellectual or literary validity. The three positions that need to be discussed are best illustrated with one major intervention each: (a) Alan Gribben's 'Introduction' to the NewSouth Edition of the book; (b) Michiko Kakutani's response to the excision of the N-word in 'Light Out, Huck, They Still Want to Sivilize You'; and (c) Toni Morrison's 'Introduction' to the 1996 Oxford University Press edition of *Adventures of Huckleberry Finn*.[12]

---

[12] All references to these texts and to *Huckleberry Finn* are from Robert S. Levine, gen. ed., *The Norton Anthology of American Literature*, shorter ninth edition (New York and London: W. W. Norton & Company, 2017).

Gribben, in the NewSouth Edition, excises the N-word, and argues strongly in favour of this editorial intervention, noting that it 'possessed, then as now, demeaning implications more vile than almost any insult that can be applied to other racial groups' and that this affront had gained rather than lost its impact over the years.[13] Both these points are thoroughly valid. Randall Kennedy at the start of his extensive study of the N-word in his book *Nigger* asks such questions rhetorically: 'Why does nigger generate such powerful reactions? Is it a more hurtful racial epithet than insults such as kike, wop, wetback, mick, chink, and gook?'[14] As his illustration of the history of 'nigger' goes on to indicate, the word obviously packs a far greater charge of devaluation, oppression, and insult than the ones he mentions.

Hence, one can understand why Gribben excises the N-word, without necessarily considering it the best option. He bases his decision to substitute 'slave' for 'nigger' on the fact that, writing in the 1870s and 1880s, Twain 'scarcely had to concern himself about the feelings of African-Americans or Native American readers', but that this is no longer the situation. He echoes, and refers to, James S. Leonard's opinion in 2001: 'The racist language and unflattering stereotypes of slaves in *Huckleberry Finn* can constitute real problems in certain classroom settings.'[15] His choice of 'slave' was influenced by the fact that, as David L. Smith put it in a paper published in 1992: 'Twain uses "nigger" throughout the book as a synonym for "slave".'[16] Moreover, it has to be noted that Gribben's decision to make this switch reflects his appreciation of Twain's novel as a text that should be taught in American classrooms minus the N-word. Obviously, he does not share the position of the educator, John H. Wallace, whom he quotes neutrally as denouncing Twain's novel as 'the most grotesque example of racist trash ever written'.[17]

The opprobrium over Gribben's excision of the N-word from the text sometimes had racist or white supremacist moorings. These are not necessarily the same things. The racist is likely to claim that

[13] Ibid., 302.

[14] Randall Kennedy, *Nigger: The Strange Career of a Troublesome Word* (New York: Vintage Books, 2003), 3.

[15] Levine, *Norton Anthology*, 303.

[16] Ibid., 297.

[17] Ibid., 303.

'nigger' is an appropriate word, for that is what African-Americans are. The white supremacist might find other ways to justify the word, including the option of racism quoted earlier, but their anger arises from a feeling of 'how dare they?' 'How dare they take such liberties with an American classic or American history?' There is also a third option in this rubric: a dishonest denial of the history of 'nigger', by reading it as 'innocent' from a white perspective and not as offensive and insulting from a Black perspective.[18] Perhaps it is only this third perspective that needs to be countered, before I return to my main argument, and move on to Kakutani and Morrison.

As Kennedy notes, 'nigger' is derived from the Latin word *niger* meaning the colour black. He quotes the *Random House Historical Dictionary of American Slang* to the effect that:

> [I]t did not originate as a slur but took on a derogatory connotation over time. ... In the 1700s *niger* appeared in what the dictionary describes as 'dignified argumentation' such as Samuel Sewall's denunciation of slavery, *The Selling of Joseph*. No one knows precisely when or how niger turned derisively into nigger and attained a pejorative meaning. We do know, however, that by the end of the first third of the nineteenth century, nigger had already become a familiar and influential insult. ...
> In *A Treatise on the Intellectual Character and Civil and Political Condition of the Colored People of the United States: [A]nd the Prejudice Exercised Towards Them* (1837), Hosea Easton wrote that nigger 'is an opprobrious term, employed to impose contempt upon [Blacks] as an inferior race. ... The term in itself would be perfectly harmless were it used only to distinguish one class of society from another; but it is not used with that intent. ... [I]t flows from the fountain of purpose to injure'.[19]

After that, Kennedy provides such a gory and shocking list of the racist, injurious, demeaning, abusive, and offensive use of 'nigger'—seldom just as a synonym for 'slave'—from the highest to the lowest

---

[18] I need to add a personal note here: the use of a word like 'nigger' can *never* be innocent. The claim that it is innocent is simply not tenable. However, whether it cannot be used at all in certain contexts, which essentially highlights the lack of innocence of its use and provenance, is another matter altogether.

[19] Kennedy, *Nigger*, 5.

strata of white society, that one needs to suffer from a particular kind of advanced myopia to see the word as innocent or even as simply an accidental insult.

However, as I have noted earlier, there were other ways in which one could, legitimately and without directly or indirectly falling prey to racism (also as noted earlier), object to Gribben's censorship of the N-word. I use 'censorship' for 'excision' to underline a core aspect of this position, as expressed in Kakutani's rejoinder in the *New York Times* in 2011. Kakutani begins by stressing the iconic status of Twain's novel. To do so, she quotes Ernest Hemingway who had stated that *Huckleberry Finn* was the fountainhead of all modern American literature. Questioning the tendency to ban, bowdlerize, and bleep—her words—*Huckleberry Finn*, Kakutani correctly notes that the N-word 'which appears in the book more than 200 times, was a common racial epithet in the antebellum South, used by Twain as part of his character's vernacular speech and as a reflection of mid-nineteenth-century social attitudes along the Mississippi River'.[20] She switches then to a critique of the censorship of books, 'removing books from the curriculum', a little unfair to Gribben's purpose, which, as I have noted earlier, was to keep *Huckleberry Finn* on the curriculum by excising the N-word. However, a point Kakutani makes about such censorship also applies to the excision: '[I]t relieves teachers of the fundamental responsibility of putting such books in context'.[21]

Kakutani then moves on to a harangue on intellectual property, which does not concern us here, and can be debated in many ways. What does concern us is her identification of Gribben's editorial intervention as a version of the 'sivilizing' that Huck is fleeing from: the act of a censoring 'Big Brother' protecting the 'naïve, delicate reader'.[22] She rails against 'political correctness' and warns that 'the language police are staging a comeback'.[23]

In short, sheared of the verbiage, Kakutani's position is that the language of an author as expressed in their text, needs to be protected for

---

[20] Levine, *The Norton Anthology*, 304.

[21] Ibid.

[22] Ibid., 305.

[23] Ibid.

historical, pedagogic, intellectual, and sociopolitical reasons. (The fact that she alludes to 'intellectual property' brings in an ideological-legal dimension too, but, as I said, we are not concerned with it here.) Interestingly, Gribben's excision of the N-word is also justified on historical, pedagogic, intellectual, and sociopolitical grounds. He wants to correct a great historic and sociopolitical injustice and abuse, and provide students with pedagogic and intellectual equipment to resist such abuse and, hopefully, reduce its recurrence in the present. If one chooses on the basis of the grounds given, one essentially has little objective choice: one will inevitably adopt a subjective position, in most cases unconsciously. In this, Kakutani and Gribben share solid grounds, which are not available to racists and white supremacists, whose positions can be dismissed objectively (and that is the reason I have not wasted much time on them).

How does one settle this stand-off between Kakutani and Gribben? As this stand-off is in the township of a book, the only way to do so—and the only legitimate way to settle such stand-offs—is to walk into the dusty alleys and crowded saloons of this town. The township of a book, as I have already noted in this book, contains alleys and houses that can be folded on top of each other. This can be done physically in ways that e-books still do not enable. But it can also be done in the imagination. And, as a novel, the word 'imagination' takes on an additional burden in *Huckleberry Finn*. Being a novel, it is, as would be said, a work of the imagination, more accurately a work of fiction. In short, nothing that is narrated in the book actually took place.

But if that is so, why does one not say that *Huckleberry Finn* is not true? Why does one not say that it is, to use an expression commonly employed these days, 'fake news'. While a handful of people might be inclined to take that option, most would flinch at the injustice of calling it—or any novel—simply 'false'. In the case of *Huckleberry Finn*, it can be argued—as, implicitly, Kakutani does in her argument for retaining the N-word—that this is a novel aiming at verisimilitude.

Observe that this argument would not cease to apply if one were discussing a work of science fiction or speculative fiction: such novels would need to aim to convince the reader that, given the context/setting, all the incidents, relations, and dialogues in the novel could, or even *would*, take place. Even the most surreal novel is based on a version of verisimilitude and/or internal laws, even if that is the exact reverse of 'normality'. But in the case of *Huckleberry Finn*, as Kakutani rightly notes, it is even more obvious: Twain could not make the characters in his novel, set in that age and place, avoid using 'nigger' and still achieve the much-needed quality of verisimilitude.

However, the matter is more complex than that: it is in the nature of the L-word, literature qua literature, to create tensions in the depiction of reality, as Plato saw a long time back. Remember that Plato's dismissal of literature was based on that perception. He had noted that an 'inspired poet is forced . . . "his profession being mimesis", while creating people who are set against one another, "to speak frequently contrary to himself". Dramatic characters take opposing sides and state contradictory ideas'.[24] The tension highlighted by Plato is imbued in literature at two levels: the level of the forms and content of literature, as Plato noted, and the level of the material of literature, as I keep insisting. This 'material' brings us to the second L-word of this chapter: language. And it is this L-word that is a problem for both Gribben and Kakutani, but in very different ways.

Gribben notes that all L-words change and are contentious, and that their meanings affect reality. He argues that the N-word is like that too: its meanings are so disturbing, its usage so destructive, that it needs to be replaced now, more so because, unlike in Twain's time, the readership of American literature has become somewhat inclusive today and the horrors of the word can no longer be ignored. Kakutani argues that all L-words change and are contentious, and so is the N-word, but replacing it avoids making teachers face up to the issues its usage encapsulates, at least historically, and imposes the censorious control of another, new set of L-words. She suggests that the only way to resolve this stand-off is to look at the ways in which L-words, which include the N-word, are used in Twain's novel, because change and contention are inherent in language.

It is easy—sometimes a bit too easy—to absolve Mark Twain. In a superficial way, it can be pointed out that his personal stance was that of an enlightened White Man, and that he was resolutely opposed to slavery: a position that he adopted with greater conviction with the

---

[24] Nickolas Pappas, 'Plato on Poetry: Imitation of Inspiration?' in *Philosophy Compass* 7/10 (London: Blackwell Publishing, 2012), 669.

years. This autobiographical reference seems very weak to me, partly because it does not look at the book in question and partly because any person's conscious position might not entirely reflect his unconscious or subconscious prejudices. Of greater use is an examination of what the words of his text convey.

There is no doubt that the N-word is pejorative today and that it had a strongly pejorative connotation in Twain's time too. It was definitely not just a substitute for 'slave', and Twain knew this very well, even if Huck might not have known. Just the way Twain makes his characters use 'nigger' indicates this knowledge. Again, Jim was not the only model available to Twain: he could very easily have written a novel with a protagonist like the erudite and impressive author and abolitionist, Frederik Douglas. But that was not the kind of novel Twain wanted to write, for a set of reasons, many of them having to do with the fact, as noted by Gribben, that he knew his target readership was almost entirely white. Not just white, but fairly privileged—or it would not have been reading novels—and, hence, it was slave-owning or had a recent memory of owning slaves. In any case, it was likely to believe strongly in stereotypes about 'niggers': giving them a character like Douglas would have cut no ice.

The fact that Twain was aware of this is indicated by the very start of the novel. It is accompanied by two pretexts, the first 'authoritative' and the second 'authorial', which subtly annotate each other. The first one, titled 'Notice', warns, adducing a great external authority, that readers trying to find a 'motive', 'moral', or 'plot' in the novel will be prosecuted, banished, or shot. The tone of this 'Notice' is mock-serious. The second, a studious 'Explanatory' by 'The Author', stresses the author's experience and knowledge of the dialects and circumstances being narrated, and ends by noting that the characters in the novel talk a bit differently from one another. Yoked together, these two pretexts are fascinating: the first mock-authoritative one dismisses the use of anything remotely like experience, reducing everything to fun and chance, while the second studious authorial pretext stresses the complexity of experience and planning that have gone into the novel. This, in general, is a tactic that Twain employs all through the novel: it calls upon the reader, or the subtle reader, to read between the lines. What the text says and what it shows are not always the same. What one character says and what that or another character does often differs. The contradictions, inconsistencies, and, above all, silences of the text contain stories too. Twain is doing exactly what offended Plato, but he is doing it to communicate what cannot be communicated easily to many of his readers. At its simplest, it can be called the gap between language and reality. Twain proves, like all great writing does, that Plato is wrong in assuming that '[t]he poet does not know "whether these, or the others, of the things said are true"'.[25] And because the 'poet' does know, in ways that are difficult to typify, or because the poet writes in such a way that the reader, then or later, can read more into the contradictions highlighted by Plato, because of that complex activity no work of literature qua literature is 'fake news'.

One can see that the N-word is necessary for this complex endeavour too, and not just for the sake of verisimilitude. To ensure this, Twain has employed another device: a first-person narrator, Huck Finn. But Huck is not just any first-person narrator: he has been carefully calibrated to bring out the tensions between language and reality. For one, he is white. Secondly, he is not an adult. Thirdly, he enjoys the privileges of being respectably white, but comes from a much more precarious background, and hence remains suspicious of being 'sivilized'. Huck is just as precisely limited a character and narrator as Jim, who is often made to speak and act in stereotypical ways.

Except that these stereotypical ways are given from the perspective of Huck, a white boy with ingrained attitudes to 'niggers' (whom he considers irrational, emotional, and unreliable, like most white people of his time) and slavery (which he does not question). The narrative of the novel reveals that Huck's and white society's use of 'nigger' is not at all innocent—for the signifiers (as adduced earlier) attach to the signified to create a sign that is obviously at variance with the referent in this novel. As many critics have noted, while looking at what Jim actually does or thinks, despite how he is (stereotypically) reported by Huck, one encounters a person who is caring, committed, perceptive, intelligent, and courageous. He arguably remains the *only* truly admirable adult male in the novel, though he is never presented as admirable. Huck's language—his L-words and the N-word laced with prejudices and stereotypes—prevent that. If this happened just once or twice, one could consider it a fluke. But as it happens again and again, and as the very structure and form of the novel aids it, one cannot but observe the ghost of Twain flitting behind the narrative being provided by Huck.

This is not to say that Twain cannot be faulted. For instance, Julius Lester correctly notes in a paper published in 1984 that it 'defies logic that Jim did not know Illinois was a free state' and that a runaway slave would 'sail south down the Mississippi', when actually the only route to freedom pointed north.[26] One can claim that, for some peculiar reason, Jim was ignorant of these facts. But to expect one to believe such a claim is to buy a dominant liberal white perception of slaves just petitioning and waiting for good-hearted whites to free them. One knows now that this was not the case: slaves were acutely aware of what was happening around them; they exchanged information all the time and often organized when they could. Such a slip is a slip, and it is necessitated by the storyline Twain needs to further his narrative, and by his readership: had he been writing for a Black readership, this would have shown clearly as a slip. In such cases, credibility is predicated on readership—and that, obviously, is also the underbelly of the use of the N-word. Twain, it should be noted, is part of that very readership: coming for a white, slave-owning background.

On the other hand, to return to Lester's critique from 1984, one cannot talk of credibility or Twain's 'contempt for Blacks', as Lester does, because Jim is a plaything, or an excuse, in Tom Sawyer's words, for 'the adventure of it'.[27] Here we return to the contradictions noted by Plato. Yes, for Sawyer, Jim is just an adventure, but then for him, as the novel shows, Huck is also an adventure. It is in keeping with Tom's very privileged background that he can afford to experience the precariousness of others as opportunity for adventure. One has already experienced some scales of moral blindness in Huck, though by the time Tom enters the narrative, that is, at the end of the novel, they have partly fallen away. Huck's blindness is largely the result of imbibing white public opinion about 'niggers' like Jim; his experience of Jim destroys most of them. But Tom's moral blindness is that of sheer privilege: life simply does not threaten him the way it threatens Jim

[26] Levine, *The Norton Anthology*, 295.
[27] Ibid., 296.

or, to a lesser extent, Huck. This too, like the contradictions between Huck's use of the N-word and Jim's acceptance of the n-role, on the one side, and the actions of Jim, on the other, is not just a fluke. It is Twain, limited as he is by his own experiences (who is not?), calling upon the reader to read between the lines, to excavate the silence, to exceed the noise, to think for themselves.

Toni Morrison, whose great novels, especially *Beloved*, are themselves brilliant examples of the capacity to write with and beyond language, sees exactly this when she notes:

> [T]he books that academic critics find consistently rewarding are works only partially available to the minds of young readers. *Adventures of Huckleberry Finn* manages to close that divide, and one of the reasons it requires no leap is that in addition to the reverence the novel stimulates is its ability to transform its contradictions into fruitful complexities and to seem to be deliberately cooperating in the controversy it has excited. The brilliance of *Huckleberry Finn* is that it *is* the argument it raises.[28]

This, then, is the reason one does not have a character based on Douglass and one has not only the N-word, but a plethora of prejudices and stereotypes about Jim; it even helps forgive, though not erase, the genuine slips that Twain, given his readership and himself, makes. These slips and usages do not detract from his main purpose in this novel: to use the language available to him in order to go beyond language and raise an argument that needed, perhaps still needs, to be made in the active spaces between L-words and N-words. This is the reason why *Adventures of Huckleberry Finn* belongs, indelibly, to the realms of literature.

---

[28] Ibid., 301; italics in original.

3

Literature, Gaps, and Ahistoricity

Very few critics would dispute what I did in the previous chapter, even if they disagree with my specific reading. That is so because my argument, as a critic, remained centred on what was said in Twain's novel, with the addition of what was just as important, perhaps more important, but had mostly stayed, in my understanding, in the gaps, silences, and noises of the words on the page. There are, however, other gaps and silences that can be excavated. I will call them ahistorical ones, because the historical context and the historical text do not obviously call for their archaeology. Now, while I insist that there are correct and incorrect readings of literature, it is also important to illustrate that 'correct' readings are not simply historically bound. There can also be valid ahistorical readings, for, as I noted in an earlier chapter, the reader and the reader's different space/time can do something to the words on the page too. Literature can, at times, allow this to happen. And this is also part of the very nature of the language of literature qua literature, an illustration of how that language differs in its very purpose from the language of other disciplines. The agnosticism that literature inculcates also legitimates some seemingly 'ahistorical' readings. Just as fiction is not fake news, such ahistorical readings are not incorrect, *per se*, and neither do they necessarily do violence to the primary text. The language of literature is not an authorial dead-end. It exfoliates with the reader—and critic—too, if deep attention is paid not just to the words on the page, which is essential, but also to the gaps between them.

To illustrate this, I will now provide a thoroughly 'ahistorical' reading of Shakespeare's *Hamlet*, a reading that, I am certain, neither Shakespeare nor any of his contemporaries would have given to the play. However, my reading is not a free play of words; I argue that,

Literature Against Fundamentalism. Tabish Khair, Oxford University Press. © Tabish Khair (2024). DOI: 10.1093/oso/9780198919582.003.0004

from our space of observation, the text actually encourages such an 'ahistorical' reading, as against many other possible readings.

By putting these two 'historical' and 'ahistorical' agnostic readings of gaps, silences, and noise next to one another in succeeding chapters, I hope to suggest how works of literature go beyond what they say, without ceasing to say something or turning into babble. Paying attention to literature enables us to see the limitations and possibilities of both historicity and ahistoricity; it makes us read meanings and significances that will be erased on either of the two sides. Paying attention to literature teaches us to distinguish not just between news and fake news and between truths and falsehoods, but even understand, for that is central to the endeavour, how and why fiction is not fake news, not even when the reader can at times legitimately change its significances.

Ophelia as Collateral Damage

Of the three arguably 'mad' characters in Shakespeare's major tragedies—Lady Macbeth, King Lear, and Ophelia—it is Ophelia who comes across as the slightest. On the other hand, it is also only Ophelia whose madness has nothing to do with her own actions. Even if one adopts a harshly censorious attitude to her daughter-like obedience of her father's advice to rebuff Hamlet's advances, it has to be noted that Hamlet has already determined, having met his own father's ghost, to play mad, and hence he has set in process the madness of Ophelia without any action on her part. Interestingly, it is at least partly the infidelity of Hamlet—who relentlessly accuses women, including Ophelia, of infidelity—that causes her madness. She herself causes nothing to happen, except of course the physical act of her (suspected) suicide. There is something very ineffectual about Ophelia's madness. Its circumstances and consequences are almost entirely confined to herself, a very private and quiet self, especially when compared to the public and very loud enactment of Hamlet's madness.[1]

[1] All references to the play to William Shakespeare, *Hamlet: Revised edition*, ed. Ann Thompson and Neil Taylor (London and New York: Bloomsbury, The Arden Shakespeare, 2006/2018).

Sandra M. Gilbert and Susan Gubar are concerned with the nine-teenth century in their seminal book, *The Madwoman in the Attic*, and hence have only three passing references to Ophelia, but they do note that Lear's madness is 'gloriously universal', while Ophelia's is 'just pathetic'.[2] At the same time, it cannot escape the reader that Ophe-lia goes mad in a play whose eponymous hero goes about *pretending* to be mad. The ease with which Hamlet's heroic enactment of madness overshadows Ophelia's real madness in the play, effectively pushing her to commit suicide offstage, has to be scrutinized, more so because later theory too, as Jacques Lacan inadvertently demonstrated and Elaine Showalter appropriately critiqued, does something similar.

In this chapter, I will look at Hamlet's enactment of his mad-ness, and Shakespeare's enactment of Ophelia's madness, and make an 'ahistorical' point that would have been far from Hamlet's com-prehension, which would also not have been part of Shakespeare's intention, but which cannot help striking any contemporary reader. In anachronistic terms—those derived from current discourses—the point is about the nature of (white) male privilege and power. To de-velop this point, one needs to present a kind of comparative study of Hamlet's play(ful) madness and Ophelia's real madness.

Foucault notes that well into the eighteenth century, even when the 'age of reason confined' various kinds of deviant people— blasphemers, spendthrift fathers, prodigal sons, the debauched, lib-ertines, the suicidal, etc.—it made 'no sign of differentiation' between these and the insane or the 'completely mad'. In Shakespeare's *Hamlet*, in a very different sense, there is 'no sign of differentiation' between Hamlet's play(ful) madness and Ophelia's real madness. Or is there?[3]

If 'the savage danger of madness is related to the danger of the pas-sions and to their fatal concatenation',[4] then, obviously, both Hamlet and Ophelia have a different relationship to the 'passion' of love and sexual attraction. Hamlet demands a kind of fidelity that goes beyond the body, and consequently accuses women of generic infidelity. His

[2] Sandra M. Gilbert and Susan Gubar, *The Madwoman in the Attic: The Woman Writer and the Nineteenth-century Literary Imagination*, first published 1979 (New Haven: Yale University Press, 2002).

[3] Michel Foucault, *Madness and Civilization: A History of Insanity in the Age of Reason*, Trans. by Richard Howard (London: Routledge, 1967/1997), 65–70.

[4] Ibid., 85.

great act of fidelity is to the memory (and the ghost, but the memory comes before the ghost in the play) of his father, but this presumes—even imposes, in Hamlet's view—the rejection of the living Ophelia, not to mention his guilty-by-mere-inference mother, Gertrude. Despite Hamlet's much-vaunted to-be-and-not-to-be-ing, the prince is guided by not just an almost demonical sense of revenge—he does not murder his uncle when he can because he wants him not just dead, but irretrievably damned—but also a strong instinct for self-preservation. This contrasts not only to Ophelia's inability to preserve herself, but also to Laertes's bold and risky invasion of the palace to seek justice after the homicidal death of his father. Ophelia seems, in this light, to be almost the antithesis of Hamlet: she obeys her father, as she should; she loves Hamlet, as she should; she is torn apart by both Hamlet's inexplicable rejection of her and her father's needless death (at Hamlet's hands), and she is unable and unwilling to preserve herself. Hence, she kills herself, while Hamlet does not kill his uncle and anyone else—except Ophelia's father by mistake in an uncharacteristically rash moment—until he knows that he is himself going to die, and then he literally, directly or indirectly, litters the stage with other dead bodies.

Despite these major differences in the way Hamlet's play(ful) madness and Ophelia's real madness relate to the 'danger of the passions and their fatal concatenation', they share a certain (dis)similarity of language. If, as Foucault notes, language was considered the 'first and last structure of madness' well into the age of reason, then obviously the occasional contextual incoherence of the language of 'mad' Hamlet and mad Ophelia demonstrate their insanity, but, in Hamlet's case, there is (famously) the hint of a 'method in his madness'. This is partly the method of language, for instance, when Hamlet instructs the players about what to enact and what to say.

The threat of suicide (by drowning, in particular) and madness has already been evoked by Hamlet's good friend, Horatio, and related to the ghost ('it'), even before Hamlet determines to play mad:

> What if it tempt you toward the flood, my lord,
>
> . . .
>
> And there assume some other horrible form
> Which might deprive your sovereignty of reason
> And draw you into madness? . . . (1.4.69–74)

Dreams, illusions, spectres, and voices in the head, as Foucault also notes, were considered a 'kind of madness of the physical world', and Hamlet and his companions are, right from the start, aware of this danger. It is suggested that the ghost of Hamlet's father—like the visions that the weird sisters make Macbeth see—could be devious and deceptive. Hamlet tries to ascertain the nature of the ghost before trusting it. But the option of self- or demonic deception would still remain a valid one in the play if it was not for the direct confessions of guilt by Claudius. This introduces a possibility/problem that we need to consider.

It appears that all three of the earliest texts of *Hamlet*—including the shortest Quarto 1 (1603) and the longest, almost twice the length, first Folio (1623)—include the confessions by Claudius. Without these, one's entire reading of Hamlet and Claudius would shift, as C.P. Cavafy brilliantly explores in his poem, 'King Claudius' (Published 1970). However, not writing as a poet, I follow the three early editions (and Shakespeareanists) in assuming that Claudius's confessions were and are an integral part of the play as written by Shakespeare, and in that case Claudius's crime of fratricide cannot be denied. This still leaves us with the possibility that Hamlet goes at least partly mad, perhaps under the impact of the ghost's revelation. This possibility, however, does not change the tenor of my discussion here. Marianne Novy notes: 'If [Hamlet] is pretending to be mad, he is deceptive on a larger scale; if he is really mad, then he is changeable on a larger scale [than the women he accuses of infidelity]'.[5] We still need to engage with the differences between Hamlet's play(ful) madness and Ophelia's real madness: What is it that makes Hamlet do (and not do) what he does, and what is it that leads Ophelia to die quietly offstage?

One obvious answer, suggested by Gilbert and Gubar, is 'female nature' as perceived by Shakespeare and/or his audiences. Phyllis Rackin has even argued that, contrary to the common assumption, 'Shakespeare's representation of women often seems less sympathetic than those of other playwrights working at the same time'.[6] But even in general, 'true' female nature, as some critics have noted, was

[5] Marianne Novy, *Shakespeare and Feminist Theory*, first published 2017 (London and New York: The Arden Shakespeare, 2019), 27.

[6] Phyllis Rackin, *Shakespeare & Women*, first published 2005 (Oxford: Oxford University Press, 2013), 48.

considered to be essentially docile and weak: even Lady Macbeth, who consciously militates against this 'nature', succumbs to her guilt (and perhaps turns mad), while Macbeth, being a man, marches on to his doom without any such show of weakness. From there, of course, one could go on to the general—and justified—point that the female is often constructed as a lack in relation to the male, just as Eve was supposed to have been carved out of Adam's rib. The hyper-femininity of Ophelia, as presented by Shakespeare, has been noted by critics too: Showalter, for instance, quotes Bridget Lyons on the extreme symbolism of Ophelia's presentation in the play, and highlights Gaston Bachelard's reading of the symbolic connections between women and death by water, arguing that for Elizabethans, Ophelia's madness would be diagnosed as 'erotomania', or 'female love-melancholy'. I find this a perfectly valid line of explanation, but I am more interested in tracing what happens between Hamlet and Ophelia, and around them, when their madness is enacted in the play. To my mind, these are the essential differences between the two:

1. Hamlet's madness is at least partly play(ful), while Ophelia's is real.
2. Hamlet's play(ful) madness is enacted throughout the play, ending in his dramatic death onstage; Ophelia's is mostly enacted offstage, ending in her quiet death.
3. Hamlet's madness impacts many other bodies, while Ophelia's only one body: her own.
4. Hamlet's madness has consequences for other people and the state at large; Ophelia's madness is apparently inconsequential, because even Laertes's bid to seek revenge on Hamlet has other causes.
5. Hamlet's madness is presumed on the infidelity of others, particularly his (guilty) uncle, (not guilty) mother, and Ophelia, and it leads him to act in a highly deceptive manner. Ophelia's madness arises from her fidelity to others, particularly her father and Hamlet, and Hamlet's highly 'theorized' infidelity to her.

All these differences undergird an obvious fact: it is not the nature of madness that matters in Shakespeare's play; it is the status and gender of the person who claims to be or is mad. Hamlet, because he is a man and an aristocrat, has literally the entire world as his stage. Ophelia is neither royalty nor a man—it has to be noted that her father's suspicion of Hamlet's initial interest in her arises because of this difference too. Seen along those lines, the play becomes a study of the relationship of madness, real or pretended, to power.

If the element of power is introduced, then we have in Hamlet not just a clear division between the 'ordinary, female madness' of Ophelia, which can only be hastily concluded, and the 'privileged, male madness' of Hamlet, which can be powerfully played out, but also a division between a madness beyond reason and a 'reasoned madness'. Foucault, writing about a period two centuries after Shakespeare's time, points out how in the eighteenth century madness is finally defined as 'being irreducible, unbearable to reason'. Interestingly, though, in Hamlet we have a play(ful) madness that has 'method' in it and that is thoroughly reasoned—not only in its causes, but also its purposes. And we have a real madness that slips out of the confines of reason altogether, just as the one it afflicts disappears and dies offstage. It is the 'reasoned madness' that is devastating: this is the madness of power, of a privileged male character. It is this reasoned play(ful) madness that has public consequences; Ophelia's madness only has a private result. Shakespeare's play never loses sight of this fact.

Rackin suggests that the gender disparities we often perceive in Shakespeare's plays have at least as much to do with us as they have to do with the playwright's age:

> The patriarchal fantasy played out in *The Tempest* has proved much more attractive to modern scholars and theatre audiences than any of the other late romances, all of which include more, and more powerful, roles for female characters. Our paradigmatic Shakespearean tragedy is *Hamlet*; it is interesting to contemplate the ways our picture of women's place in Shakespeare's plays would be altered if it were *Antony and Cleopatra*.[7]

In that light, perhaps our continued focus on the 'existential' questions raised by Hamlet's tragedy—and so loudly announced by him onstage—is at least partly a reflection on us and our inability to

[7] Ibid., 51.

disentangle 'existence' from power, particularly the power of (white) male privilege. To me, the unquestioned status of male privilege as enacted by Hamlet comes across not only in the visible staging of his play(ful) madness, its disastrous public consequences, and our tendency to highlight its existential aspects, but it also comes out, grotesquely and painfully, in Ophelia's burial scene. Ophelia has just died offstage, driven mad by the death of her father and Hamlet's taunts and 'reasoned mad' infidelity. She is said to have committed suicide, but King Claudius and Queen Gertrude have managed to arrange a quiet burial for her in sacred grounds, despite some whispered controversy. Her brother, Laertes, has returned, to mourn both father and sister. Along comes Hamlet, making 'existential' comments about life, death, and privilege—comments of a sweeping nature, not very different from his comments on the infidelity and carnal nature of women during his last meeting with Ophelia—and his first act of any real consequence until then is to *compete* in grief with Laertes. Even if one assumes that Hamlet is not aware of Laertes's identity when he (Hamlet) steps forward and questions his (Laertes's) despairing act of jumping into Ophelia's grave—after Laertes has vigorously defended the 'angelic' nature of his sister against the insinuations of the officiating priest—it is clear that even afterwards Hamlet is competing in grief with Laertes and everyone else:

> I loved Ophelia—forty thousand brothers
> Could not with all their quantity of love
> Make up my sum. . . . (5.1.256–8)

Both Claudius and Gertrude see this as an act of madness, and Hamlet's exaggerated vaunt of grief for the death of a woman whose 'life' he shunted into a 'nunnery' during their last meeting and whom he has not given much thought to after that, does have an element of madness:

> 'Swounds, show me what thou'lt do.
> Woul't weep, woul't fight, woul't fast, woul't tear thyself,
> Woul't drink up easel, eat a crocodile?
> I'll do't. [. . .] (5.1.274–7)

But if it is madness or even the extravagance of grief, it is also the empty vaunt of entitlement: today, one would like to ask Hamlet to go ahead and eat a crocodile.

No one, it appears, is allowed to feel as deeply as Hamlet. Just as no one is good enough to marry his mother—that is his only actual complaint against her, for there is no reason to suppose that she even knows about Claudius's crime and every reason to suppose that Claudius is a good husband—no one is good enough to grieve over the woman he loved, not even her brother. In the nature of power, the private (as Ophelia) is finally 'collateral damage' to Hamlet—obsessed as he is with the murder of his father, the noble king, and his replacement by the 'ignoble' uncle. In the nature of entitlement, everything—even the death and grief of others—is of a secondary nature to one's feelings of privilege. Hamlet might not have imagined the ghost of his father, but he does imagine things about other people—not least the generic infidelity of Ophelia—and the nature of his male privilege not only allows him to act on his assumptions, but also causes irreparable, 'collateral' damage to those around him, close by or, as in the case of Rosencrantz and Guildenstern, far away. His privileged obsession with his own rights and wrongs, his unending existential dilemma, is literally the death of others. Shakespeare might or might not have had all this in mind, but it is surprising that even today we tend to think of and teach *Hamlet* along 'existential' lines even as the story is just as much, if not more, about power and male privilege. It tells us much about our own age, an age that has finally found a term for the murder of the private by the public, of the ordinary by power and entitlement: *collateral damage*. But it also suggests a 'gender- and power-based' failure on our part to contextualize the language and silences of the text.

Summing Up This and the Previous Chapter

In conclusion, eschewing tenets of criticism and theoretical formulations, and basing my discussion on readings of literature to the extent possible, I have, in this chapter and the previous one, tried to illustrate how both historicity and ahistoricity can be part of critical responses to literature but are not sufficient to defend or critique literature, or even its readings. This, however, I have argued does not mean that they do

not exist. I have used a/historicity as a convenient catchword to gesture at the various critical schools that privilege or disparage social,
political, gendered etc. readings of literature today. There are critics
who dismiss the very category of literature as a universalist concept,
arguing that essentially anything is literature; there are critics who talk
about the school of resentment, dismissing recent theoretical and political interventions in literature. My position is that both sets of critics
are like the proverbial blind men giving us a description of the elephant. Literature—because of the ways in which it uses language to
negotiate reality, as I have been illustrating in this book—escapes their
strictures.

The contexts of writing and reading *Huckleberry Finn* have changed,
as has the text (or its significances, as indicated most obviously by the
shift of significance of the n-word) and this has resulted in a different relationship between contexts and texts, and this difference can
neither be ignored nor used to erase the precarity of other meanings.
I have tried to indicate that the text—what it says, what it does not
say, what it cannot say—of *Huckleberry Finn* allows us to read it in ways
that enrichen rather than impoverish its meanings and significances
despite, or perhaps even because of, this historical change. The historicity of the text is vital to this endeavour, this reading, but it is
historicity situated in different ages, places, and circumstances: most
obviously, that of the writing and that of the reading. On the other
hand, in *Hamlet*, I have advanced a reading that is essentially ahistorical. But it is not ahistorical as a free play of ideas, an arbitrary
imposition on the text of *Hamlet*[8]: the text and its gaps actually allow
such an ahistorical reading. This enables us to release meanings and
significances that have nothing or little to do with the intention or even
historicity of the writing, but are vital from the space of its reading, in
this case, my post-Iraq War space. This reading, while ahistorical, is
not an imposition, for the text of *Hamlet* allows a new concatenation
of meanings and significances now.

Just as what literature says is absolutely vital (the words of the text
have to be read), its historicity—both of writing and reading—can

---

[8] By 'arbitrary', I mean, for instance (if I may be allowed to be facetious), a reading of Prince Hamlet as actually a space alien in camouflage. Whatever might be the
intellectual joys of such a reading, it would not be a reading of *Hamlet*.

never be ignored. But finally, literature goes beyond the historical limits of words too, by providing space for noise, gaps, silences, etc. The complexity of reading that this requires—and that can only be learnt by reading literature as literature—is essentially what frightens fundamentalists, with their streamlined notions of truth and falsehood. The growing inability to *read* literature as literature translates into a growing inability to read the complexities of the world—of 'reality'—and explains much about cries of fake news and post-truths.

4

Language, Literature, and the Book

In his autobiography, *Les Mots* (1964), Jean-Paul Sartre recalls the time when his mother started reading stories out to him, similar to the ones she had already been *telling* him in the past, but without the aid of a text until then.[1] He used to love those pre-text stories, with their 'half-completed sentences', 'slow-to-come words', and 'brusque confidence, quickly defeated and put to rout, which disappeared with a pleasant fraying sound, and then re-established itself after a silence'. But when she began to read out the stories, something strange happened. This is how Sartre recalls it:

> Anne-Marie made me sit down in front of her, on my little chair; she leant over, lowered her eyelids and went to sleep. From this mask-like face issued a plaster voice. I grew bewildered: who was talking? About what? And to whom? My mother had disappeared: not a smile or trace of complicity. I was an exile. And then I did not recognize the language. Where did she get her confidence? After a moment, I realized: it was the book that was talking.[2]

From a writer who displays an almost Proustian ability to circle around the same event or statement and reveal it as slightly different with each shift of angle, Sartre's account subtly reveals the differences between the spoken word and the written word, and suggests how the artificiality of the book is also its strength when it comes to literature.

---

[1] Some portions of this section in this chapter are based on and/or extracted from an essay that I contributed, while working on this book, to an anthology. See Susheila Nasta, Ed., *Brave New Words* (London: Myriad, 2019).

[2] J.-P. Sartre, *Words*, first published 1967, trans. Irene Clephane (London: Penguin Books, 2000), 31.

Literature Against Fundamentalism. Tabish Khair, Oxford University Press. © Tabish Khair (2024).
DOI: 10.1093/oso/9780198919582.003.0005

Literature, for my generation, was primarily words on paper—though both the screen and audiobooks have started changing this now. But even before my generation, and many generations before it, came to read words on paper (and, further back, on parchment, stone, clay, etc.), we were already surrounded by words in the air—and these words continued to surround us down to the generations of paper, and will continue to envelope the coming generations, even if they migrate entirely to another medium of reading, such as the digital screen. Language is the term we use to talk about all these words, though obviously there is a difference between what is spoken (but not read), what is spoken because it is being read out, what is read but not necessarily spoken, and what is read on paper or on, say, a computer screen. Common lore holds that this 'language'—which changes in so many contexts—is nevertheless a distinctive and unitary feature of humanity.

However, some might argue that not just other animals and birds have a 'language', so do fungi—if one is thinking of signals that help in basic communication.[3] It seems fair to assume that systemic sounds were being made, including by our ancestors, before language evolved among human beings about half a million years ago, and that these sounds served the purpose of communicating in that hoary past as well. Does this kind of 'communicating' include a basic level of 're-membering' (and, hence, at least the possibility of 'storytelling'): so that when birds remember the sequence of possible decay in the food they bury, are they actually following acoustic and other signals from around them, signals that determined their sequence of burials initially too? There is a difference between communicating and thinking, and one that in some ways also explains the difference between the hesitation and doubts that Sartre heard when his mother was thinking up a story to tell him, and the confidence he sensed when she was reading out a story.

So, do other animals *think* in language too? In order to answer this question, one needs to compare someone shouting a sudden 'boo!' behind them to someone saying 'vampire!' in a lonely, dark place. The reaction, for the faint-hearted, might be similar, but it does appear to

[3] Merlin Sheldrake, *Entangled Life: How Fungi make our Worlds, Change our Minds, and Shape our Futures* (London: The Bodley Head, 2020).

me that a loud 'boo' is closer to a signal, while 'vampire' is a sign. If that 'vampire' was part of a story being told to them, they would obviously reach another layer of complexity. Even if, being a staunch animal lover, one wants to insist that the sounds non-human animals make constitute thinking in a language too, at least it can be said that human animals take this to a very high level of complexity and abstraction. As far back as the first decades of the twentieth century, Russian linguist Lev Vygotsky was essentially making this point when he argued that inner speech is not just a version of ordinary speech, but has its own patterns, and that it is this inner speech that makes human thought possible.[4] The issue of whether thought comes first or speech had been considered in the nineteenth century too, and this controversy rages even today, though often in different terms.[5] Without settling it in favour of either side, one can simply accept that thought and language are indivisible in human beings, and that acceptance would be sufficient for my purpose.

Bear in mind that thought does not exhaust the human experience. For instance, one has emotions, feelings, etc., and these are not thoughts. However, once one starts thinking about them, one ends up using language.[6] This complexity has created many problems, not least in Freudian psychoanalysis, which are only recently being addressed.[7] For instance, is it possible to simply talk repressed traumas from the past into healing, or does the language of that discourse shape, alter, even create feelings, emotions, experiences which were not there? Once again, one need not take an extreme position on this side or that, but it would be a rash psychologist who would not be

[4] Lev S. Vygotsky, *Thought and Language*. Revised and expanded edition. Ed. Alex Kozulin, trans. by Eugenia Hanfmann and Gertrude Vakar (Cambridge, MA: The MIT Press, 2012).

[5] See, for instance, the different positions adopted by various leading linguists in Anjum Saleemi, Ocke-Schwen Bohn, and Albert Gjedde, Eds., *In Search of a Language for the Mind-brain: Can the Multiple Perspectives be Unified?* (Aarhus: Aarhus Universitetsforlag, 2005).

[6] So the quandary arises: You can experience an emotion without thought, but can you *know* what you experience without thought? In other words, the emotion is 'named' only via thought and hence language. There is always, as both poets and philosophers have known, a 'shadow' that falls between the name and the named, the signifier and the signified. Many shadows, actually.

[7] Daniel Adleman and Chris Vanderwees, *Psychoanalysis and the New Rhetoric: Freud, Burke, Lacan, and Philosophy's Other Scenes* (London and New York: Routledge, 2022).

aware of the fact that language, when used to examine what does not exist in language, when used even to simply 'think' about it, can effect whatever it is that might have existed. German physicist Werner Heisenberg's uncertainty principle is, for once, useful to recall outside the field of quantum physics in this case. Again, the easy recourse in some circles to evolutionary theory as explaining cultural behaviour is faulty from this perspective: a 'boo' is not the same as a 'vampire', and the threat of a snake is not the same as the snake in Eden, and, through complex and culture-specific transference, the 'slimy devilish foreigner'.[8]

Thought does not exhaust human experience, but thinking in language does effect and define it in complex ways—ways that change with the medium of language even if and when the words stay the same. Hence, the word on paper is the same as the word that is spoken. And yet, when the writer, so to say, plucks the word out of thick air and puts it down on paper, an incredible change has taken place. In literature, we can trace this change in so many ways. The age when words used to exist in air is almost a separate planet from the age when words started getting pinned down on parchment and paper. We look back from our age to the previous one and think that we can still breathe in their words, partly because some—the Odyssey, the Mahabharata, etc.—have survived (or so it seems) and partly because some 'tribes' with little or (at least until some decades ago) no writing still exist.

But, alas, the words deceive us. Or they deceive us because we wish to be deceived. Because all those ancient 'untexts' contain glaring clues about their difference which are ignored. We attribute them to authors, we squabble to turn them authoritative, we annotate them as texts. We forget that the moment an 'oral text'—an oxymoron—is put down on paper, its words become something else. Even if we imitate the structure of an 'oral text' in writing, we use words differently.

---

[8] Even the evolutionary experience of fearing snakes, which is a valid factor, is insufficient on its own to explain why snakes, especially the highly poisonous king cobra, are worshipped, fed, and considered essentially benign by many Hindus. A discussion of this might take one into matters like the 'holy terror'—the relationship between the sacred and the terrifying—that Terry Eagleton discusses in a book, but that in itself would be a cultural matter, a matter of signs, a massive complexity of signs, and not of mere signals.

Compare the Australian poet Les Murray's excellent 'The Buladelah-Taree Holiday Song Cycle' (1977) to the Aboriginal 'songs' it builds upon. Even though these songs, once written down, have already become something else than simply oral, they still differ from Murray's poem in significant ways. For instance, Murray can replicate their repetitiveness and circularity—essential for mnemonic purposes in oral compositions—but he cannot make his song contain the information and work directions that Aboriginal song cycles do. One does not need Murray's poem to have even a holiday—itself a concept worth examining—but the Aboriginal song cycles were needed to specify routes, record ancestries, even erect shelters.

This is not Murray's fault. Something happens when the word is plucked from thick air and pinned on paper: Literature comes into being. The author—who can now be authoritatively discussed (or dismissed)—can choose to collect information and 'facts', or do something else with words. In due course, one inevitably talks of medical literature and other disciplinary literatures on the one side and literature on the other, which might partake of medicine or history or philosophy, but works both with and outside their disciplinary demands on language. This different approach to what can be done with and in language enables, among other things, the language of literature to keep changing shape without becoming shapeless, to keep shifting significance without becoming meaningless.

To some extent, the young Sartre noticed this difference between the stories his mother told and those she read out to him. For the word has changed—turned flesh—not only at the moment of its being written down; it is a change that percolates down to the reading. It is the same word yet entirely different—and one is not even talking of changes in meaning because of time or space! The book that talks through the mouth of Sartre's mother speaks another language. Every book turns its reader into an exile—and books of literature use this too.

The huge planetary distance between orality and literacy, between untexts and texts—a distance that is largely ignored—haunts even the reading of 'texts'. And yet it is a different kind of haunting, which comes with many advantages. For, to interpose from Sartre, one learns to speak in tongues! Who is reading, Sartre wonders, when he hears his mother read. Who is speaking, we wonder, when we read a book.

Who is thinking, and how, one might also ask, when any 'story' comes to us from someone else, or through a given medium, or is mediated by us to someone else.

Thinking in language is at the core of the need for literature to think beyond language. This is a complex matter, and I only want to delineate its many possibilities with just one example of possible processes: that of 'efference copy'. In *Other Minds*, Godfrey-Smith brings up the idea of 'efference copy' in two different contexts.[9] First, in Chapter 4, he introduces the idea, without naming the concept, to explain 'how evolution created new kinds of loops between action and the senses'. As he explains it later in the book, animals capable of movement have to 'deal with the fact that what they do affects what they sense'.[10] Efference copies are used to provide the brain with a template of evaluation of action and result: did I move my eyes, or did that bush I moved my eyes over also move? When I pushed this chair, did it move as it would have, or is it on rollers, or tied to the floor? Godfrey-Smith explains the process in these words:

> With an efference copy mechanism, as you decide to act, sending a 'command' of some sort to your muscles, you also send a faint image of the same command (a 'copy' of it, in a rough sense of that term) to the part of the brain that deals with visual output. This enables that part to take into account what your own motions are doing.[11]

However, it is not this version of efference copies that interests me primarily in this book. Its other use—this time named as a *concept*—occurs in Chapter 6, when Godfrey-Smith is essentially discussing language. This follows a longer discussion, relating to the egg or chicken matter of whether thought came first or language, which he wisely settles by pointing out that in any case language is essential to complex thinking. He does offer the usual examples of animals capable of complex thinking, such as chimpanzees stacking boxes to reach a fruit, or birds

[9] Peter Godfrey-Smith, *Other Minds: The Octopus and the Evolution of Intelligent Life* (London: William Collins, 2018).
[10] Ibid., 144, 144–5.
[11] Ibid., 144.

remembering not just where they buried food, but also which pile would decay first.[12]

To me, it seems to be sheer sophistry to deny that language—an abstract, vocalized, and later inscribed system of symbols and signs—is not a dominant part of thinking among human animals, and that it is lacking in non-human animals, though its absence might well have accentuated other forms of thinking in them. My position on the role of language is stronger than Godfrey-Smith's. But his moderate position can be accepted for this book: 'Language provides a medium for the arrangement and manipulation of ideas.'[13]

How does it do so? It is here that efference copy steps into the discussion, with reference to a longer debate about the nature of 'inner speech', that is, when one talks to oneself. Godfrey-Smith notes that speech is a planned action, and all of us desire to achieve a degree of precision in achieving our speech objectives. You want an apple and not a pumpkin, when you ask for an apple.

Godfrey-Smith notes:

> In speech, the creation of an efference copy enables you to compare your spoken words to an inner image of them; this can also be used to work out whether the sounds 'came out right'[. . .]. Ordinary speech involves, in the background, a kind of internal quasi-saying and quasi-hearing [. . .]. Once we are generating these nearly-spoken sentences to check what we actually say, it's not too big a step to put together sentences that we don't intend to say, sentences and fragments of language that have a purely internal role. The forming of sentences in our auditory imagination creates a new medium, a new field of action. We can formulate sentences and experience their results. When we hear—internally—how some words hang together, we can learn something about how the corresponding ideas hang together.[14]

[12] One could add to these examples from books like Peter Wohlleben's *The Inner Life of Animals* (2018), where, among other examples, one encounters the possibility of horses feeling shame.

[13] Ibid., 145.

[14] Ibid., 145–6.

If one were to put this extract against Plato's objections about the contradictions contained in a literary work, then it would become clear how literature works in and as language, and also beyond it. The language of literature can be seen as a particularly fruitful and fraught relationship to and of efference copies. Every slight shift in the material of language—ranging from a new word of slang to the growth of complex ideas (or even change of the context of its utterance or reception)—can induce a different relationship between what is being uttered and what is being thought. The fact that these two will never be totally identical in any complex linguistic performance (that is not simple mimicry[15]) also opens up the options of what cannot be said. The very disjunction noted in the first use of efference copy— between action and result, between output and input, between sense and sensed—is part of this equation too: there is always a shadow that falls between thought, word, and action, so to say.

The language of literature is always double-sided. In literature, the double-sidedness of language is not just that of 'what I want to say' and 'what I actually said'. It is also, and here I lean more towards Vygotsky, that of 'what I said' and 'what it enabled me not to say'. Which inevitably opens up other areas of double-sidedness: 'what I said' and 'what I thought', or 'what I thought' and 'what I said', or 'what I could say' and 'what I might have said', or 'what was said' and 'what was heard'. Replace that 'I' with a narrator or a character, and the possibilities and combinations explode. No wonder, Plato took the shortcut of banning the poet. Maybe he might have suggested executing the poet if he had thought of readership, another explosion of combinations, as we do today! Because the 'book' adds to this double-sidedness, while at the same time providing us with a medium that accentuates and enables, in Byung-Chul Han's words, the 'deep attention' or 'contemplation' that distinguishes human culture.

Literature is not, as Murray discovered, about passing on useful facts to other individuals. The untext—when it existed before writing became prevalent—had to do so. It had to combine the emotive, imaginative, formal, and other skills of what is today called literature

---

[15] One wonders about the insistence on parrot-learning at the heart of various religious traditions.

to record and convey useful mundane facts: lineages, routes, hunting lore, foundational myths, building techniques, pairing rituals, etc. But the very fact of words becoming flesh[16]—on paper—has split them, slowly at first, and with greater acceleration later on as writing spread and became easier to reproduce. Now there are words that give facts and information, and . . . and what?

And there are similar words, the same words, often exactly identical words, that refuse to be pinned down. The words of literature are not *different* from the words of medical and other literatures, which is why there was once the *need* to demolish the capital 'L' of literature. And, of course, all these words are not different from the words that hover in air all around us, the words of our speech, breath-words.

Words that have been penned down have not really been pinned down. If the text can never be the untext, there are things that the text can do which were not possible for the untext: it can split up words. Or maybe, words in a text can split themselves up. So, there are the words in the book read by Sartre's mother, there are the words released by her into thin air, and there are the words heard by Sartre. And, actually, for this accounts for the difference Sartre notices, there are the words he has heard elsewhere or earlier. They are all the same words, and they are not the same words. The authorship of literature is deceptive and its readership disruptive: this is partly due to the connected and separate acts of plucking words from thick air and putting them down on paper and, in another year or space, releasing them from paper back into thin air.

Later in the autobiography the young Sartre learns to read like all of us—what he feels he should read, what he has to read, and what he likes to read. More than that, he reads in texts what his grandfather or his mother does not read in them. The text exposes the disjunction that the presence of the utterer often hides, though it exists in any use of language: 'The worst of it was that I suspected the grown-ups of play-acting.'[17] This is an ability of the text that the untext could not have to the same degree, for the untext had only one enunciation in the present.

---

[16] D. H. Lawrence in his unused forward to *Sons and Lovers* insists that really the flesh is made word, which might actually bring us to the same point.

[17] Ibid., 54.

The fact that there are so many different versions of oral untexts (like the earlier stories of the Mahabharata) often fools us—textual paragons that we are—into assuming that the untext, on its own and in its instance, contained multiple meanings. This is misleading. The untext did not have a text against which it could be compared, and hence it could change across time and space. Meanings could accrue to it across time and space, as a consequence. But these were not the meanings in its instance of enunciation in a particular setting. Far from it. Because it did not have an authoritative text, it needed to be enacted and learnt by heart, so that in any specific social context, its words were fixed and unchanging. A large degree of agreement was demanded for its very survival. The untext could have only one rendition at a time—and its speaker and listener were joined by common sociocultural bonds. Let me adduce just one historical illustration:

> The Rig Veda was preserved orally, but it was frozen, every syllable preserved for centuries, through a process of rigorous memorization. There are no variant readings of the Rig Veda, no critical editions or textual apparatus. [. . .] In contrast with the Rig Veda, [The Mahabharata, which was preserved both orally and in writing] changed constantly; it is so extremely fluid that there is no single Mahabharata; there are hundreds of Mahabharatas, hundreds of different manuscripts and innumerable oral versions.[18]

For dissent to survive, if not exist, oral communities would require large segments of support. Individual dissent might exist, but would never be recorded or preserved in purely oral societies. It would die out without the support of a community. One needs writing for it; one needs a book. Imagine a singer in an oral society composing a song of strong dissent. A Boris Pasternak, a George Orwell of orality. What would happen to them? What would happen to their song? Would they be allowed to sing it? Would anyone in that society—full of people who disagreed with them—want to learn it by heart, so that it could be passed on to the next generation?

[18] Wendy Doniger, *The Hindus: An Alternative History* (Oxford: Oxford University Press, 2009), 33.

The text—by trapping words—also frees them. Academics frequently exfoliate aspects of this basic fact: intentional fallacy,[19] death of the author,[20] reader response theories,[21] distant reading,[22] etc. Various devices associated with literature, such as the use of irony,[23] or the free indirect style,[24] also essentially explore the existence of the same thing. The fact is rudimentary: the word, plucked out of thick air, and made flesh on paper, will one day be read and released into thin air. Sartre and his mother. More interestingly, unlike the untext, the text will be read 100 kilometres away or 50 years later 'as it is'—and its words will again be released into thin air. One understands where the religious might have got their hopes from: the spirit is made flesh in the text, and then it is released again and again into all eternity. Except that each release is different—it changes eternity, it changes the word made flesh, and it changes the spirit behind it all.

Reading a word is not the same as speaking it; it never was and never will be. Hence, disciplinary literature does its best to contain the words it uses. It does not always succeed; some of the words, sooner or later, rip themselves away, change into something else; for instance, turn into noise (jargon), or lapse into silence (redundancy). But disciplinary literature does its best, as it should. It plugs the gaps and goes on: alchemy becomes chemistry, Newton shrinks to accommodate Einstein, natural selection is buttressed with genetic mutations.

The rise of writing—in Harari's terms, a full script and not a partial script (which, like numbers, cannot be used to write poetry)—further increases the possibility of contemplation—across time and space—and contracts its applicability at the same time. This Harari (and others) have noted too:

The most important impact of script on human history is precisely this: it has gradually changed the way humans think and

[19] W. K. Wimsatt and Monroe C. Beardsley, *The Verbal Icon: Studies in the Meaning of Poetry* (1954) (Lexington: University Press of Kentucky, 1982).

[20] Roland Barthes, 'The Death of the Author', in Roland Barthes, *Image, Music, Text*, trans. by Stephen Heath (London: Fontana Press, 1977), 142–8.

[21] Iser, *ibid*.

[22] Franco Moretti, Distant Reading (London: Verso, 2013).

[23] Clare Colebrook, *Irony* (London: Routledge, 2003).

[24] James Wood, *How Fiction Works* (London: Picador, 2018).

view the world. Free association and holistic thought have given
way to compartmentalization and bureaucracy.[25]

This is actually what I also say when I note the 'disciplinary' uses
of language: why I argue that academic disciplines, including literary criticism, are necessary but not sufficient to deal with literature.
Literature, as this book tries to illustrate, resists this compartmentalization and bureaucracy of language, and even employs *script* to
do so.

Literature learns—or at least its handful of real practitioners
do, despite what its publicists, agents, and editors might choose to
promote—to live with brave (new and old) words. The bravery of
words is also the bravado of books. This 'bravery' exists on the page
before it comes to exist elsewhere. Something has changed not just
when the untext became a text; something also changes when the
word is pinned to a page. To say that it dies would be a mistake. It
changes, just as for the religious the soul does not die when it is im-
prisoned in flesh for the duration of a lifetime. The word that existed
in the air—in the age of the untext or of the text—was always the
same word. Its utterance, as Valentin Voloshinov or Bakhtin might
have put it, determined its meaning.[26] This meaning, as Bakhtin suggested, was monoglossic—one can say, in a simplified manner, that it
was fixed by the context.[27] I could shout 'idiot' to a rash driver, and it
would be a word of hatred and aggression. I could say the same word
smiling and softly to my gambolling child, and it would be a word
of love and approbation. In either context, it has only one meaning.
That, however, is not the case when the word 'idiot' is written on paper and left lying about. What are its meanings? Does it have any
meaning? What noise does it create? What blank silence envelops it?
Dialogue, for Bakhtin, means not just two people talking, as it does
in ordinary speech, but 'communication between simultaneous differences'.[28] 'Double voicing' is essential to Bakhtin's reading of language

[25] Harari, *Sapiens*, p. 146.

[26] V. N. Voloshinov, *Marxism and the Philosophy of Language*, first published 1929, trans.
Ladislav Matejka and I. R. Titunik (Cambridge and London: Harvard University Press,
1996).

[27] Bakhtin, 'Discourse in the Novel', in Bakhtin, *The Dialogic Imagination*, ibid.

[28] Katerina Clark and Michael Holquist, *Mikhail Bakhtin* (Cambridge; MA: Harvard
University Press, 1984), 9.

in writing.[29] This aspect of *difference* cannot be evaded in writing, as it can be, given physical and social imposition of power, in the flesh.

One is reminded of the word 'harlot' written in 'big, staggering letters' on a chit of paper in Chekov's story. The bravado of combustible books allows the bravery of words. It allows, or at least furthers, the possibility of agnostic reading demanded by literature. Whether this will survive the new modes of reading that computerization is bringing in its wake is a moot question, but not the purview of this book. Let us, instead, in the next chapter, look finally at this matter of agnosticism with reference to belief or disbelief in God, for it has a direct bearing on my discussion of literature and my argument that literature is the antidote to fundamentalism.

[29] For a complex discussion, which goes far beyond my simplified presentation above, refer to Charles Lock's 'Double Voicing, Sharing Words: Bakhtin's Dialogism and the History of the Theory of Free Indirect Discourse', in *The Novelness of Bakhtin: Perspectives and Possibilities*, eds. Jørgen Bruhn and Jan Lundquist (Copenhagen: Tusculanum, 2001), pp. 71–87.

5

Fundamentalism, Literature, and God

In an anthology of papers titled *Islamic Fundamentalism*, the editors note a startling fact.[1] While Muslim societies have thousands of commentaries on the Quran written in the past, contemporary Islamists in the twentieth and twenty-first centuries have seldom engaged with their holy book: 'In fact, apart from al-Maududi (d. 1979) and Sayyid Qutb (d. 1966), there is hardly any significant work by Islamists in this regard.'[2]

In retrospect, this is not surprising: *fundamentalists are not interested in multiple readings or even discussions of their sacred stories.* They insist on *one* interpretation.[3] Their insistence is partly necessitated by the fact that their 'literature' has slipped from orality into literacy—the text, the book. The simplistic 'postcolonial' celebration of oral cultures as spaces of multiplicity is blind to the fact, noted in the previous chapter, that the transmission of knowledge, images, information, thought, ideas, opinions (as forms of what we later term 'literature') in any specific oral culture is based on a large degree of social hegemony. True, the lack of an 'authoritative' text might create different versions of the same story over large spaces and periods of time, but this is not the case in any specific time and space: versions of 'priesthoods'

---

[1] This chapter is partly based on an essay that I wrote defending the concept of 'god' from an atheistic perspective. It appeared the *Economic and Political Weekly*, India.

[2] A. S. Sidahmed and A. Ehteshami, eds, *Islamic Fundamentalism* (Boulder, CO: Westview Press/HarperCollins Publishers, 1996), 3.

[3] Unlike what writers sometimes think (as, for instance, Salman Rushdie does in his portrayal of the uber-fundamentalist, Khattam-Shud, in his delightful novella, *Haroun and the Sea of Stories*), religious fundamentalists are not opposed to the 'imagination'. Actually, their religious world is populated with the imaginary. What they have problems with is a reading that changes with contextual alterations, and with multiple or even just differing readings.

Literature Against Fundamentalism. Tabish Khair, Oxford University Press. © Tabish Khair (2024).
DOI: 10.1093/oso/9780198919582.003.0006

determine what is transmitted and how. It is, hence, not surprising that the requirement to control meanings and readings came up only years after the initial oral 'revelation', when the Quran was codified and organized into a book. It was not that such a requirement was not implicitly in place to some extent earlier on; it is just that it was not consciously and structurally required: sharing the same cultural space sufficed in primary or even, at times, predominant orality.

The increased insistence of religious and other fundamentalists on singular, or at least delimited, readings of their sacred texts, now written down, comes from this change, and, in that sense too, it is a modern, technological, and disciplinary development. Just by the fact of being written down, their 'literature' has escaped the kinds of control that are 'naturally' put in place during oral transmissions in societies of primary orality, and at the same time it has also become accessible to other kinds of formal controls. This includes the insistence on authoritative readings, authoritative iterations of the text,[4] totally ahistorical or narrowly historical contextualization of the text, controls over translations, a narrow priesthood-scholarship of accredited commentaries, etc. A transparency and unilaterality of meaning/interpretation is demanded on the one side, and anything that does not fit this paradigm is false or meant to be left obscure (and, hence, not subject to any interpretation, let alone various ones). As Fahad Khosrokhavar notes, 'But to them [Jihadists and Islamic fundamentalists], the Koran and the Prophetic traditions (sunna) are transparent, and entirely clear at their core, and the parts of the Koran that are incomprehensible to them are also impenetrable to [all] other human beings. There is no other valid interpretations than theirs.'[5]

If fundamentalists even engage with a different reading, and they do so very rarely, it is to dismiss the other reading. Islamists, for instance, do not want you to discuss the Quran openly; they want you to accept it as interpreted by a particular 'sanctioned' scholar or, at most,

---

[4] Interestingly, even a religious complex like Hinduism, with its many sacred texts and many versions of the same sacred texts, partly due to their long oral roots in a large culturally and linguistically diverse space, has faced a similar problem. Take for instance, the recent Hindu fundamentalist backlash against the scholar and poet, A. K. Ramanujan's discussions of the various extant versions of the *Ramayana.*

[5] Farhad Khosrokhavar, *Jihadist Ideology: The Anthropological Perspective* (Aarhus: Centre of Studies in Islamism and Radicalisation, Aarhus University, 2008), 93.

a particular school of scholars.[6] I highlight the Quran in this context, not because this happened only with that book—it is a common feature of religious fundamentalist readings of revered texts in other religions too. However, perhaps, this raid of the 'language police' on the Quran is particularly revealing of the general fundamentalist attitude to texts, because, in the Quran, 'language is of central importance': Mustansir Mir notes that the Arabs were fiercely proud of their linguistic prowess—the word 'Arab' literally means 'the articulate', the non-Arabs being called 'Ajam', literally, 'the dumb', and that the Quran, proclaimed to be the only miracle of the prophet of Islam, managed to finally convince 'non-believing Arabs' at 'the level of language or form' rather than 'that of content or message'.[7] 'What initially impressed the Arabs was the Quran's literary beauty, which eventually led them to accept the Quran as divine revelation.'[8] This slippage from the literary qualities of a 'religious' text to a disciplined policing of its meanings is, as I propose here, the distinguishing characteristic of all kinds of religious fundamentalism. Hence, the problem of defining religious fundamentalism—an impossible mission if based

[6] In a religion like Hinduism, this does not seem to be the case, but it is deceptive. Hinduism is not a religion primarily based on divine texts because it has too many of them. But it is, in its dominant Brahminized forms, based on a strong social construct. Hence, the rigidities insisted on by Hindutva fanatics are social and historical: the very definition of what is 'Indian' these days. The common argument that Islam is more intolerant than Hinduism is based on a blindness to this, despite the evidence of caste intolerance in Hinduism. The fact remains that both Islam and Hinduism, like all other religions, are tolerant in some and intolerant in other ways. In short, if Islamic fanatics tend to be intolerant of those outside the faith, but theoretically consider those within the 'true faith' to be equal, Hindu fanatics were, until recently, perfectly willing to ignore whatever existed outside the Hindu fold, but strongly invested in maintaining the social (both gender and jati or caste) hierarchies within it. Both positions are inherently limited: the Islamic fanatic is forced, because of his rigidity of definitions, to constrict the scope of 'true faith' with time and space, so that increasingly they end up fighting other Muslim groups too. The Hindu traditionalist was faced with a lack of cohesion to oppose external threats *and* oppression within the fold, to maintain its structure, especially in terms of caste. Hindutva, as it exists today, is both the consequence and an attempted solution to this problem: it works by including the 'outcastes' as much as possible (but without questioning the caste system), and simultaneously imposing the intolerance of the traditional Brahminical Hindu social structure on non-Hindus, especially Muslims, by reducing them to second-class Indian citizens, where the definition of 'Indian' has already been monopolized.

[7] Mustansir Mir, 'Islam', in Felch, ibid., 233–48, 233.

[8] Ibid.

on definitions of religion or deity, which often vary extremely from one another, as Cicero had his commentators note more than 2,000 years ago in *The Nature of the Gods*—is not a theological or philosophical matter; it is a *textual* matter.

This problem is confined not just to religious thinkers, but also crops up elsewhere. For instance, Plato's problem was not that the world is too much with us; it was that there is far too much of the world. His Socratic dialogue with Ion is intended to prove two things: that Ion, as 'rhapsode', or for our purpose a 'creative writer', cannot claim to be an expert on a poem (in this case, Homer's) and that, in any case, Homer's work is just an accumulation of copies of copies of the real ideas/forms.[9] This profusion of second-hand copies in poetry, which, as Plato argues in the *Republic*, was morally dangerous, was poised against a unitary 'ideal'. The poet not only failed to access this ideal, but actually moved in the opposite direction towards multiplicity, contradiction, 'falsehood'. For one, the poet set out to copy the reality out there—all those different chairs—and hence was twice-removed from reality, the chairs being themselves once-removed from the actual 'reality' of the ideal chair.[10] This is what, in literary criticism, is referred to—and sometimes critiqued—as Plato's theory of 'mimêsis', or imitation, mimicry, representation.

This is partly a simplification of Plato. Plato did not see poetry only in terms of imitation and representation, even though that is his default position. The very fact that he exiled the poet with a heavy heart indicates his recognition of something beyond superficial mimicry in the artistic process. Nickolas Pappas notes that Plato develops a theory of 'artistic inspiration' in a section in Book 4 of his *Laws*, and

[9] Plato, *Ion*, in Hazard Adams, Ed., *Critical Theory Since Plato*. Revised edition (Fort Worth: Harcourt Brace Jovanovich College Publishers, 1992), 12–17.

[10] A necessary clarification: the word used by Plato, *eidos*, is translated as both 'idea' and 'form' in English. But in ordinary spoken English, 'form' is opposed to 'idea'. Not only is form connected to material existence and experience, the same idea can take many forms. The 'form' Plato meant can be better understood as 'archetype'. Before going further, let it be clear that Plato did not use 'eidos' in the modern sense of forms, but to suggest 'ideal/archetypal form' and/or 'absolute idea'. And he was convinced that this eidos could not come from experience—or living in the world. Instead, it was eidos that shaped our experience. This was so because, at its simplest, experience was physical (visible), multiple, transient, and changing, while eidos was immaterial (invisible), unchanging, and eternal.

probably only in that text.[11] However, Pappas continues to paraphrase the Athenian Stranger in Plato's *Laws*:

> An inspired poet is forced … 'his profession being mimesis', while creating people who are set against one another, 'to speak frequently contrary to himself'. Dramatic characters take opposing sides and state contradictory ideas. The poet does not know 'whether these, or the others, of the things said are true'. Lawmakers must not be permitted to make legal pronouncements in the same way.[12]

Pappas notes that it is striking that here in the *Laws*, Plato 'pits poets against legislators, considering that the *Meno* finishes by conflating the statesman, oracle-chanters and soothsayers, and every breed of poet. We call them all "divine" and "divinely inspired", Socrates says.'[13] But the point that is of relevance to us is the fact that Plato, almost against his natural inclination, has to insist on disciplining the representation of reality in language, and he realizes that this is not what the writer of literature can or will do.

It is in this sense that the need to discipline language into one meaning—'divine' for the religious; 'ideal' for Plato—leads to a common suspicion of the poet, while also, at the same time, an use of the 'tools' of the poet. Many religious texts and all the works of Plato, and many other philosophers, ranging down to Karl Marx, are highly 'literary'. (For me, as implicit throughout this book, such texts can also be 'literature'.[14]) This again becomes a problem for those of their followers who want to control the meanings—and readings—of the text. Not necessarily the religious followers, but always the fundamentalists. And this applies not just to religious matters, but also to philosophical, political, and economic matters. So that a fixed interpretation of, say, Marx or Lenin is a form of political fundamentalism, and a rigid adherence to certain texts and precepts of, say, capitalism is a form of economic or political fundamentalism. In all these cases,

---

[11] Pappas, 'Plato on Poetry', 669.

[12] Ibid.

[13] Ibid., 670.

[14] Unsurprisingly, the narrator-protagonist of Teju Cole's novel, *Open City*, is a Nigerian psychiatrist, working in post-9/11 USA, who reads Sigmund Freud largely as poetry.

the stress is on a selection of texts, icons, or principles, and, even more so, on a certain delimited way of reading those texts, icons, and principles. Alternative readings are not considered options to be discussed—and perhaps objectively evaluated—but simply wrong or false.

Similarly, while sacred texts of all religions contain elements that some would find problematic, it is not the texts themselves that are a problem, for, in almost all cases, the problematic elements can be excised in effect or at least explained away as no longer applicable. This, it needs to be added, was the version of believing Islam—both my parents were believers—that I grew up with in a small town of India: matters like polygamy, purdah, over-strict halal observances, rote rituals, etc., were all rejected from *within* the bounds of Islam. This is usually called 'interpretation' or 're-interpretation' by the religious. Fundamentalists strictly control, mostly prohibit, this option. I saw this happening to both Muslims and Hindus around me while growing up in my small town. It was my first vague realization of the fact that it is not the texts that necessarily lead to fundamentalism, but a certain mode or ethos[15] of reading the texts. It was an ethos that insisted on fixing language—not just the language of texts, which concerns me here, but also the 'languages' of clothing, rituals, etc. It is a kind of 'disciplinary' requirement.

On the matter of Divinity, Cicero observed that, 'the pronouncement of highly learned men' are 'varied and . . . much at odds with each other', including views on whether (and why) the gods exist or not.[16] One of the sad pleasures of reading Cicero's *The Nature of the Gods* is the realization that learned discussion of the existence of God has not exceeded the parameters outlined in that book, while popular discussion is usually far from reaching those parameters. The only real development has come from the direction of science—its greater methodization has obviously impacted on the discussion.

[15] I take 'ethos'—though my earlier preference was for 'mode' and I do not absolutely abandon this harder option—from Philip Davis's *Reading and the Reader* (Oxford: Oxford University Press, 2013).

[16] Cicero, *The Nature of the Gods*, first published 1997, trans. P. G. Walsh (Oxford: Oxford University Press, 2008), 3.

Jumping the centuries, in our age the new atheists (Richard Dawkins, Christopher Hitchens, and others)—a desirable and legitimate reaction to the rise of religious fundamentalism among the masses—have taken up the existence of God, or rather God's lack of existence, with particular vigour. At its simplest, though not always, new atheism is the philosophical face of the rise of positivism in recent years. Hence, much as I welcome its pushback against religious fundamentalism, it needs to be noted that new atheism is not really a matter of doubt. One can even argue, and Terry Eagleton has suggested as much elsewhere, that new atheists are not atheists in the older sense of the word.[17] Because the atheist—or, as I prefer to put it now, the agnostic—was traditionally someone who doubted: they *could not* believe that God existed. This contrasted with the common religious insistence on belief in the existence of God. The new atheists, it appears, tend to insist that God *does not* exist. In that sense, their reaction has not just been opposite, but also apposite.[18]

Because whether one believes that God exists or not, one is still in the realm of 'belief'.[19] To say that one cannot believe in the existence of God is very different from the statement that one believes that God does not exist. Both statements—that God exists and that God does not exist—are essentially, given their unprovability, matters of belief. The inability to believe in the existence of God is a matter of honest doubt because the existence of God cannot be proved or disproved. Even science, unlike what some think, does not settle the matter for good, despite all the evidence that can be piled on the one side.[20]

There is, of course, an argument from some new atheistic quarters that my last sentence is vague or invalid. For instance, we cannot prove or disprove that a huge blue and red teapot is circling some sun of our

---

[17] Terry Eagleton, *Holy Terror*, Oxford: Oxford University Press, 2005.

[18] Some portions of this section in this chapter are based on an article that I initially wrote for *EPW*: Tabish Khair, 'Is an Atheistic Defence of God Possible?' *Economic and Political Weekly*, vol. 51, no. 14 (2016), 39–43. http://www.jstor.org/stable/44002650.

[19] The quandary that we witnessed in an earlier footnote comes up again: It might be possible to 'believe' without thought, but can you *know* what you believe without thought, and hence, language?

[20] Victor J. Stenger, *God: The Failed Hypothesis—How Science Shows That God Does Not Exist* (New York: Prometheus Books, 2008).

universe. But it is reasonable to say that such a thing is highly unlikely and anyone who expects to be served tea from this gigantic teapot is in for disappointment—and perhaps starvation. God, argues the new atheist, is like the concept of this blue and red teapot out in the universe: one cannot disprove either, but there are good grounds to believe that both do not exist.

Does it sound logical? Well, yes, but it is based on a reductive engagement with concepts of God and religions. In some ways, it engages with just the most simplistic, clerical, and ritualistic aspects of religion—and, hence, inevitably comes to share in their simple inanity. Because the point of any complex notion of God is that it cannot be equated with *anything* that we know or experience as living beings. A huge blue and red teapot is a projection of a limited human experience and that, as any complex religious thinker would tell you, is exactly what God is not![21]

From as far back as ancient Greece, apophatic theology, also known in Christian thinking as negative theology, has been a type of theological thinking that attempts to describe God, the Divine, solely by negation, because God cannot really be 'known' to humankind. To claim to know the mind of God (let alone God!) is to claim to be bigger than or as big as God, which should be blasphemous for the truly religious. The ninth-century theologian John Scotus Erigena put it even more radically:

> So God does not know of Himself what He is because He is not a 'what', being in everything incomprehensible both to Himself and to every intellect. . . . But He does not recognize Himself as being something (*Se ipsum autem non cognoscit aliquid esse*). . . . For if He were to recognize Himself in something, He would show

[21] But this also brings one back to common religious conceptions of God today—shapeless, crucified, or multi-headed—which do not seem to differ much from the notion of a gigantic teapot in space. New atheistic treatises have correctly pointed out that religions, using God as an excuse, have committed and continue to commit many evils, and that they are seldom likely to fully tolerate those who refuse to (or cannot) believe. It is also true that the claim of the religious to know the 'mind of God' is preposterous. One can argue, and mystics have often had this complaint against established religion, that God can only be a personal matter: any rule attributed to God, any claim to speak on behalf of God is not only absurd, as Hitchens would put it, but the greatest 'blasphemy against God', as some religious mystics of the past have suggested across Asia, Africa, and Europe.

that He is not in every respect infinite and incomprehensible. (*Periphyseon*, II.589b–c)[22]

Stories of *religious* personages, such as radical Sufis, insisting on this perception even at the cost of their lives, abounded in the South Asia of my childhood. In his excellent book, *The First Firangis*, Jonathan Gil Harris recounts the reported end of the Indian saint, the nude Yogi-Sufi, Sa'id Sarmad Kashani, probably born an Armenian Jew, along those lines.[23] Revered as a Sufi (Muslim) holy man by Hindus and Muslims, when asked to recite the Islamic article of faith by the authorities, Sarmad left out one phrase, thus stressing the 'negativity' of God and not rounding it out with a 'positive' statement of faith. The first article of faith in Islam states that 'there is no God, but God': Sarmad stopped after 'There is no God'. (He was reportedly beheaded for his refusal to go beyond the first phrase.)

Some branches of Hindu philosophy as well as Buddhism embrace a similar approach to God, or Divinity (which is a better word), as does the Arabic system of *lahoot salbi*, which influences some Shia and Sunni schools and defines many Sufis. None of these schools would have their faith disturbed by the argument of a roving celestial teapot, despite what it might do to the beliefs (and practices) of religious fanatics who are doing most of the shouting—and much of the killing—in the world today.

These, and similar, bits of 'new atheistic' criticism do not come fully to grip with God: they either deal with an aspect of religion, or deal with God in the reduced sense in which religious fundamentalists use the concept. Similarly, attempts to prove the existence of God also do not go very far: they are usually based on the assumption that there must be a God because there seems to be purpose and order in our universe. Evidently—in a kind of reverse version of the celestial teapot—this is based on a wafer-thin slice of human experience. Is there order in collapsed galaxies? Is there order in black holes? We

[22] Quoted from the Stanford Encyclopedia of Philosophy. Retrieved from https://plato.stanford.edu/entries/scottus-eriugena/#EriuLibeArtsMast on 27 April 2021.

[23] Harris quotes a translation of one of Sarmad's couplets, whose poetry ranges from the mystical to the profane: 'It's wrong to ascribe any miracle to the naked Sarmad/The only revelation he has made is the revelation of his private parts.' Jonathan Gil Harris, *The First Firangis: Remarkable Stories of Heroes, Healers, Charlatans, Courtesans & Other Foreigners Who Became Indian* (New Delhi: Aleph Book Company, 2015), 231.

are adducing from our own thin slice of experience on this speck of a planet in a vast and immeasurable universe. In a more limited sense, there is 'order' for us also as a species because we are thriving as a species, but is there 'order' for dinosaurs? Or, if one really looks at even our own situation again, is there order for a village being swept away in a flood? Would one be as convinced of order if they and their family were starving, ailing, and about to die every other day, as millions are in the world? They might still resort to faith to purport a Divine Order (as Job did), something larger than personal experience, something to hang on to, but then that would be belief, not evidence.

Basically, all these arguments in favour of or against God do not go even an inch beyond the point reached by Alfred Tennyson more than a century ago in these lines from poem LIII of *In Memoriam*:

> Behold, we know not anything;
> > I can but trust that good shall fall
> > At last—far off—at last, to all,
> And every winter change to spring.

> So runs my dream: but what am I?
> > An infant crying in the night:
> > An infant crying for the light:
> And with no language but a cry.

Tennyson knew (much better than current defenders of God) that he was not talking of proof; he was talking of trust in an incomprehensible universe. Faith. 'Behold, we know not anything'! He knew that any claim to scientifically prove the existence of God is basically unsustainable. All those books that believers write to provide 'scientific evidence' of the existence of God are based, entirely, on subjective and unrepeatable reports or on large inferences based on narrow experiences, or on ignoring one's own privileges. God can only be a matter of faith, of 'trust', not of science. God's existence cannot be disproved—but it cannot be proved either. About this, old-fashioned atheists were right, and both the religious and the new atheists are wrong. What I dub agnosticism in this book, and turn into a matter of reading, and reading literature, is essentially aligned to the position of these 'old-fashioned atheists', not the new atheists.

Cicero's commentator puts it with greater nuance than most believers and non-believers. Referring to Epicurus, he claims that 'gods exist because nature herself has imprinted the conception of them in the minds of all'.[24] I obviously reject this explanation not because some Oriental religions do not have a concept of God (I think they have equivalent god-functions, even when they do not have a god), but because it is obviously put in subjective terms, and depends on a deification of nature itself. The notion of a divine nature—unfortunately, a subconscious part of some scientific thinking too, including in fields such as genetics—needs to be rejected, for it essentially does not differ from the notion of God (as Cicero knew too), and remains susceptible to a similar range of objections. However, the observation made by Cicero's commentator earlier deserves close attention: one cannot assume that nature, a kind of divine architect, has implanted the concept of God in human minds, but what is known is that the concept—and its equivalents (what I have called 'god-functions')—exists in all languages.

Again 'God' cannot be justified simply because—as is obvious—the 'symbolism' of homo sapiens (a distinctive evolutionary feature, it has been argued) inevitably leads to the symbolism of religion. Because even if one argues that symbolism is essential to a distinctively human existence, one need not agree that the symbolism of God is necessary or even desirable. Human beings have been known to abandon many symbols, including entire languages. No, one has to engage with 'God' because one cannot get rid of the issues resolved within and addressed by the concept even if one truly and wholly has no belief in God, even if one lacks—and one always does so, by definition—the language to talk about 'God'. There is an experience of reality by human beings which needs a signifier like 'God', though the signifier itself, like all signifiers, is slippery and not sufficient.

Hitchens notes that man might well have made God.[25] There is solid anthropological evidence that (wo)man has made God, because the concept of God has 'developed' and changed with corresponding developments in the socio-economic and cultural environments

---

[24] Cicero, *The Nature of the Gods*, 18.

[25] Christopher Hitchens, *God Is Not Great: How Religion Poisons Everything* (London: Atlantic Books, 2007).

of human beings: that is why, as M. M. Kosambi noted decades ago, the dominance of the concept of a universal, unseen God coincides, historically, with the rise of universal currencies and universal monarchies.[26] Though, of course, the thoughtfully religious have an answer for that too: they attribute it to the developing capacity of humanity to think about what is, finally, a deity that cannot be fully grasped.[27]

If one concedes that Hitchens is right about the 'made on Earth' provenance of God, can one still argue that it is not possible for 'humans' to abandon 'God'? I would say so. 'God' is obviously a sign whose referent is not available indubitably to our other senses, and whose referent, by definition, cannot be fully comprehended by our

[26] M. M. Kosambi, *Ancient India: A History of Its Culture and Civilization* (New York: Pantheon Books, 1965).

[27] In fact, it might be appropriate to pause for a while here and look at what this historical and anthropological evidence suggests to us, and particularly to me as an Indian. Brahminical Hinduism and Judaism have their roots in cultures that either predated the establishment of universal currencies and universal monarchies, or coincided with their initial evolution. As such, while both have some notion of universality (inevitable the moment one human being recognizes another as human, or two apples from different trees as the same fruit), their cultural ethos is based on a privileging of absolute difference. Until recently at least, one had to be born a Jew to be a Jew, and even now one has to be born a Brahmin to be a Brahmin. Christianity and Islam, being later religions which evolved well after the consolidation of large universal states (the Roman Empire, for instance) with large-scale trade and universal currencies, tend towards a privileging of universality: all Christians are equal, as are all Muslims, at least in theory. What is interesting is that if a religion privileges difference, it can lead to a very strict internal hierarchy—for instance, the Brahminical version of the Indian caste system—but also very little concern with what exists outside this hierarchy, for it is conceptually excised. Hence, Brahminical Hinduism is perfectly willing to pour molten lead down the throats of offending Dalits, but quite unlikely to wage a 'jihad'. On the other hand, a religion like Islam—premised on the universality of all human beings (which is why they have to become Muslim, says the fanatic)—promises equality internally and constantly runs the risk of waging jihads externally. After all, if universality calls upon you to erase your difference, then you have to be simply forced to do so if you perversely refuse! Obviously, whether one comes from universality or difference, there is the risk of oppression, though of different kinds. One of the indicators of the human construction of religion is this: human beings need both universality and difference to be human, but religions in different periods, depending on the contexts they grew up in, have usually failed to find a working balance. The imperfection of religions, in this and other contexts, remains a good argument against their divine provenance, though it is by no means an irrefutable argument, for religious imperfections can also be blamed on human failures. (Even here, though, the notion of an all-powerful God does not mesh with the facts of human failure—because obviously any failure of God's creation is inevitably a failure of God. The religious notion of 'free will' resolves this, but only to the extent that it turns God into a bemused TV game-show host.)

human senses. 'God' comes into being in language and always exceeds what can be said in language: even the 'attributes' of God are always human attributes, in the sense that we can only understand them with human experience and examples. In short, 'God' is shifting shorthand (signifier and sign) in language for a relationship that humans have with each other, with themselves, and with the world, as well as that residue or excess of existence that the word 'human' cannot exhaust. Within all religious traditions, God stands for the index of all that humans cannot be. And God also stands for all that humans are capable of becoming.

The fundamentalist claim that one knows God so well that they can act on God's behalf is effectively the same as the claim that they are God. In almost all spiritual traditions, this claim is resisted: spiritualists and mystics usually relate to their gods only at a personal level, without making public claims about what others should or should not do. Such claims are made by those segments of the religious who wish to run a society and a state. They are claims to power. Discipline is what they want. And because they are based on the conviction that one knows exactly what God wants, they implicitly equate one's consciousness with the (unknowable) consciousness of God. We act like we are God, and hence the consequences are always disastrous.

This, obviously, also applies to scientific positions. One can see how the principles of evolutionism have been distorted in popular writing to suggest a nature that works like the mind of a knowable and purposive 'God'. One can sense the frustration in the words of scientist and science writer, Nick Lane, when he notes:

> [There] is the common misapprehension that evolution necessarily tends towards greater complexity, and that microbes, being microscopic and without brains, are at the bottom of the evolutionary pile. So many evolutionary biologists have attacked the lay concept of evolution as a progression towards a higher plane, and to so little avail, that one begins to wonder whether there is a global conspiracy to thwart them.[28]

[28] Nick Lane, *Oxygen: The Molecule That Made the World* (Oxford: Oxford University Press, 2009), 30.

What frustrates Lane is exactly this notion of a fully 'knowable, purposive' nature/God that justifies us, because he knows that natural selection is largely a random matter and the notion of the 'fittest' does not permeate from the organism to the sub-cellular levels.[29]

I am not making a mystical claim, or denying the fact that science has led and can lead to greater knowledge in particular fields. But what I insist on is the fact (bracketing the issue of language here) that every bit of knowledge gained usually leads us to some other space where knowledge is lacking. This is sometimes obscured, at least in popular discourse, because I have yet to meet a serious scientist who is not aware of the possibilities and limits of scientific knowledge. Sometimes the use of language leads to this kind of obscuration, because language needs to work with known concepts. For instance, when we are told that quantum particles are both waves and particles, we are given two known terms, 'waves' and 'particles'.[30] But, of course, whatever is being alluded to is both wave and particle, and neither wave nor particle. It is a third thing altogether, which we cannot 'name' in our spoken language (mathematics is another matter) or even really imagine given our Newtonian experience of the universe. Any attempt to forget this in the field of science is similar to an attempt to imagine 'God' as a known quantity in the field of religion. And it is exactly, as I have stated earlier, the achievement of literature to talk about a reality that *cannot be 'named'*—historically, politically, or even ontologically speaking—*while also naming the world*, or at least what can be named (contentiously or not) in the world. When I suggest that 'humans' perforce come into existence between 'beast' and 'God', but cannot be subsumed within either of these two conceptual categories without

[29] Just as there is a tendency in religion to speak for 'God', there is a tendency in science—or rather in popular renditions of science, and in attempts by scientists to procure funding or visibility by appealing to political prejudices—to claim to know the 'mind' of nature. For instance, the media discourse of the 'gene' for criminality, the 'gene' for homosexuality, etc., when every serious scientist knows that no complex trait depends solely on a single gene.

[30] From a philosophical perspective, this problem obviously replicates other, older problems, not least the dualism of Descartes, which purported a distinction between brain and mind, but could not resolve the issues arising from this separation. Cognitivism and current sciences have settled Descartes' dualism largely in favour of the brain, but the problems have not gone away.

having their humanity erased, I actually adumbrate the purpose and role of literature qua literature.

The earliest Greek comprehension of the poet—or, in the terms of our age, the 'creative writer'—is that of a kind of inspired madness. The poet is *ouk ephrôn*, not of sound mind. The 'inspiration' of Divinity that redeems the poet, at least in one of the texts of Plato, is not immaterial to this conception of literature, for it records the fact that literature can access what is not easily or entirely accessible.[31] Reading the 'madness' of both is largely a matter of language, but not only as language. The Sufi who says 'There is no God . . . ' and stops there, not completing the phrase with 'but (the One) God', is doing in and with the language of religion what the poet does in and with the language of the 'world'.[32] The presumed transparency of language is shattered with the stone of some noise, contradiction, silence, etc., which reveals the prospects of other meanings, meanings which are not transparent at that moment and in that context, and might (at times) never be transparent. To return to the Sufi 'blasphemy', it needs to be noted that the refusal to complete the phrase is not necessarily a rejection of God—as the custodians of religion supposed. It can also just be an insistence that faith is rooted in a kind of negation. The very fact that the Sufi sage uses the line from the Quran suggests this possibility: that the silence at the end of this dramatically and (for the religious) dangerously incomplete phrase is not a rejection of the Quran, but a provocation to think more deeply while using it. Surely, if the holy text were to be rejected by the Sufi concerned, he would have refused to quote from it. Instead, what he did was to quote from it in such a way that the lines were revealed as carrying other layers of meaning. One can claim, and I am sure the Sufi would have agreed, that in effect he was not reducing the Quran, but adding to its significance by illustrating its depth of meanings. But that, exactly, is what a fundamentalist cannot allow: a multiplicity of interpretation, depth of meanings. The Sufi was also, in the context of this book, reading the Quran as literature. To return to Cicero's commentator, gods are *not* implanted in human minds by nature, and hence they are not an example of

[31] Nickolas Pappas, 'Plato on Poetry: Imitation or Inspiration?' in *Philosophy Compass* *7/10* (London: Blackwell Publishing, 2012).

[32] For an interesting account, see Gil Harris, *The First Firangis*, 212–79.

prolepsis. The signifier 'God'—or its equivalents and replacements—
is a necessary function of language. I do not mean this solely in the
way in which comparative religion puts it, when, for instance, William
Paden accurately defines gods 'as instances of a form of religious language' and adds that gods are 'the points at which humans relate to
"the other"'.[33] I suggest something that is far more integral to the relationship between language and 'reality', and hence something that
is totally inescapable, whether or not one believes in God. The signifier 'God' is a bid to address something beyond language that can
never be fully encompassed in language. In that sense, it is an accented
version of what happens with *all signifiers in language*, for they do not directly and naturally 'represent' what exists outside language, either
materially (as referents) or conceptually (as signifieds). On the other
hand, they are necessary to access—and think about—what does exist
outside language.

The fact that religions that do not have 'God' do have 'god-
functions' is finally a very simple aspect of how, to refer again to
Ferdinand de Saussure, language works as a system of differences.
While this observation is sometimes taken to suggest a primacy of language as an arbitrary system—and hence, an endless 'play'—it can
be turned around to look at the materiality of what is not language.
As mentioned earlier, following Saussure, one has to note not just the
arbitrariness of language as a system of differences, but also that the
removal of a signifier in a system of differences effects all the other
signifiers/signifieds related to it. What this suggests is the existence of
a world—material and/or conceptual—of non-verbal experience and
tactile sensation, which demands to be addressed. 'God', as explained
earlier, is exactly such a signifier—a concept that enables us to address
and understand core aspects of our experience, even when it cannot
be exhaustively equated, as is demanded when literature is reduced
to reportage or thinking to fundamentalism, with a given referent out
there. This is the reason why, if the signifier God is missing in some
religions, its space is filled by other god-functions.

Here the concept of God and the signifier 'God' enter exactly the
space that the language of literature explores: that space which cannot

---

[33] William E. Paden, *Religious Worlds: The Comparative Study of Religion* (Boston: Beacon
Press, 1994), 121.

be conceptualized fully and rendered transparent or communicable in and as language. What language about such spaces demands is an agnostic reading: a reading not just of what exists in language but also of what does not, a reading that does not say 'I believe' or 'I do not believe', but stays prepared to judge contextually and constantly. Let me illustrate with an example from 'religious literature' what an agnostic defence of 'God' does to an understanding of God, and God's relations to humans, and how it is essentially a literary reading. The two cohere: the problems and possibilities of reading 'God' are the same as the problems of reading literature, and hence reading literature as literature is an antidote to fundamentalism.

The Example of Job

I was taught the *Book of Job* as literature in my small town in India (with very few Christians); *not* in the English-medium Roman Catholic school that I attended, but in the public Gaya College, where most of the teaching was in Hindi and there were hardly any Christians around. This was probably fortunate, because it is a text that, for many believing Christians, says everything about faith and belief that needs to be said. It gives all the answers that the faithful want about faith and that the devout want from God. Or does it do something far more complicated than giving easy answers? An online essay by a faithful Christian lists the following points as the lessons of the *Book of Job*:

> 1. Believe with all your heart in the absolute sovereignty of God. Pray that God would give you that conviction. 2. Believe with all your heart that everything he does is right and good. Pray that God will give you that assurance. 3. Repent of all the times you have questioned God or found fault with him in the way he has treated you. Pray that God would humble you to see these murmurings as sinful. 4. Be satisfied with the holy will of God and do not murmur.[34]

No doubt this is what the *Book of Job* says. But is it all? And is it even the most important of its 'messages?'

[34] I have not referred to the online source as the commentary was not posted as a scholarly reading, but simply as a statement of the writer's personal faith. It would be wrong to reveal their name in this critical and scholarly context.

Not only I, but almost all serious scholars of the text would doubt it. My reading of the text does not insist on exclusivity. However, what it insists on is paying closer attention to it and its contexts. This closer attention is demanded 1. by the fact that the text contains gaps and silences which evade the four lessons of absolute faith in God, and 2. by the context it was written in—let alone the various changing contexts in which it has been and will be read. I will return to these matters. However, the closer attention I demand is also predicated by the fact that the *Book of Job* is by no means the only text that proposes, in keeping with the reading, absolute trust in God. If absolute trust in God was the main and definitive aspect of this text, then there is no reason why it would have received precedence, as it has in the hands of millions of different readers across centuries, over a million other texts of faith, or, for that matter, the paraphrased four lessons listed earlier.

Let us then begin with the context of the *Book of Job* and then look at its text. Let us pay some attention to what it was meant to say (if that can be deciphered), what it said, what it says, and, above all, what it fails to say. As John Gray notes in his magisterial study, the religious, philosophical, and even textual roots of the *Book of Job*, a cornerstone of Jewish and Near Eastern 'wisdom literature', go back to Sumerian Mesopotamia and Egypt of the third millennium BCE, a period distinguished by 'scientific interest in nature and society'.[35] Apart from compiling exhaustive lists, which find a reflection in citations of God's power, etc., in the *Book of Job* the 'sages in Egypt and Mesopotamia were embarrassed by the fact that in actual experience the [Divine] Order in which they believed (and of which they saw so much evidence in nature and society) was apparently disrupted by occasional vicissitudes'.[36] In other words, the Divine Order was not always either orderly or just, or so it seemed. Mentioning another text, not familiar to me, from the same period, 'Dialogue of a Man with His Own Soul', Gray goes on to state that it is on the 'apparent lack of moral order in the world and the pointlessness of life, [and it is exactly] the note on which the Dialogue in Job opens'. He then notes that fundamentally 'the problems of

---

[35] John Gray, *The Book of Job* (Sheffield: Sheffield Phoenix Press Ltd, 2015), 4.
[36] Ibid., 7.

the writers of both texts were the same, the discrepancy between experiential facts and the Divine Order in which both believed', a discrepancy felt by writers in Mesopotamia too around the same time.[37]

By the time the *Book of Job* was compiled, '[f]aith in God's moral government and the optimism of current piety had already been questioned ... in the psalms which voice the plaint of the community or of the individual on behalf of the community'.[38] What psalms of this type, and the *Job* too, posed was a moral problem to the certainties of conventional faith. Like the Book of *Job*, they 'show concern about the suffering of the innocent and the prosperity of the wicked ... [H]owever, the moral problem is not a scandal to faith as in the argument in *Job*.'[39] In short, as Gray notes, the *Job* in its historical context was a 'challenge to orthodox belief'.[40] It took the doubts about the suffering of the innocent and posed it as a question about the nature of Divinity, or, even, the existence of a just Divine Order. In other words, it did exactly what, as we will continue to see in this book, literary texts do: it pushed language to the limits of what it could say in its period.

The *Job* offers a resolution to this dilemma, for the dismissal of God is not really an option in the text, given the fact that the story, after introducing Job in nine verses, directly features God in audience: 'Now one day the celestials came and presented themselves before Yahweh.'[41] A story that features God obviously cannot contain the premise of there being no God. What it can do is debate the nature of God and Divine Order. This is what happens in much of the book. Only when Job is finally answered by God does one move on inevitably to 'absolute faith in an absolute God', but only from a particular religious reading. Because, as scholars have noted, God does not answer any of Job's questions. Why do the just or innocent suffer? Why do the wicked prosper? What kind of God can allow such disorder in the world? To insist on 'absolute faith in such an absolute God' is

[37] Ibid., 8.
[38] Ibid., 27.
[39] Ibid.
[40] Ibid., 28.
[41] Ibid., 120.

potentially a fundamentalist interpretation. This is more so because the reader of the *Book of Job*, unlike Job, does not get to meet God face to face: a meeting that obviously mitigates the incompleteness and evasiveness of God's answers to Job by assuring Job of God's interest in him.[42]

Instead, even from a religious perspective, God does offer other answers to Job. One of them is this: the power of God cannot be understood because of the limitations of human beings. 'God does not explain or defend himself; he challenges the understanding and agility of his opponent. This aims to engender in Job a proper sense of his limitations.'[43]

These two answers are not necessarily the same. The power of God, as Islamists often demonstrate, can assume the shapes of oppression, violence, etc. But the 'limitations of human beings' is a different matter. As argued, the very notion of God—as a necessary concept, and not an entity—arises from the placement of humanity between power and limits. The definition of the human is that which is located between 'God' and 'animal'. Or as Gray puts it later in his study, '[t]he very token of the "otherness" of God and the evidences of his power and providence beyond the competence of humankind stimulate hope beyond human limitations'.[44] One does not need to believe in God in order to occupy this position *between* the human as sharing what the religious call the 'divine' and what they denigrate as the 'animal' in us. But one does need a concept of infinitude and otherness which corresponds to the idea of God, at least before it is reduced to a set of rules and rituals by the clerics of religion. This concept—word or statement—is however, as in the case of all language, neither transparent nor unchanging in its meaning and significance. For it to remain meaningful and significant, it has to be embedded in a different ethos of reading—that of literature.

---

[42] The misleading 'resolution' of the *Book of Job* seems to be a common religious closure and can be found, among others, in the deeply philosophical *Bhagavad Gita* too: Arjuna asks Krishna a number of very difficult questions, most of which are only partially answered, but then the matter is clinched with Krishna simply revealing his divine 'cosmic' shape to Arjuna. As Doniger puts it, the moral impasse and questions of the *Bhagavad Gita* are 'not so much resolved as blasted away' (Doniger, *ibid.*, 282).

[43] Ibid., 451.

[44] Ibid.

Interestingly, this is exactly the reading that some scholars have
provided of the many and disparate *stories* of the *Mahabharata*, one of
India's foundational 'epics', which essentially grapples with the matter
of dharma (in the sense of 'moral law'). Noting that the *Mahabharata*
was written down from oral roots *after* 'dharma had essentially been
somewhat codified', Doniger comments:

> 'What is dharma? Asked Yudhisthira, and did not stay for an
> answer. As one of the early dharma texts [*Apastamba Dharma Sutra*
> 1.7.20.6] puts it, 'Right and wrong [dharma and *adharma*] do
> not go about saying, "Here we are"; nor do gods, Gandharvas,
> or ancestors say, "This is right, that is wrong."' The *Mahabharata*
> deconstructs dharma, exposing the inevitable chaos of the moral
> life.[45]

The stories of the *Mahabharata* work as necessary approaches to discuss
that about dharma which necessarily escapes the languages of codifi-
cation. Ruth Vanita's *The Dharma of Justice in the Sanskrit Epics* essentially
provides a reading of the sacred Hindu epics as literature to illustrate
how they contradict or question—often in what I have termed gaps,
silences, and noises of the text—even their own (from our perspective)
unfair textual strictures about caste, gender etc.

In short, to read the *Book of Job* as giving easy answers of faith is to
read it partially. It is a bit like taking a theory and applying it to a work
of literature. But to read it agnostically as a text in *its* context and/or in
our context is to excavate many more meanings—and questions. *Book of
Job*, as literature, never lets the reader off the hook. All literature forces
the reader to take a stand, to judge, even as it exposes the *situationality*
of every stand, the limits of all judgement, the simultaneous is/isn't of
many 'realities'.

It has to be noted that the 'judgement' of literature is a direct consequence of the way in which literature is accessed, the way it exists
as literature. Let me illustrate this. I grew up in a country where people are fanatical about cricket. However, only a small percentage of
these cricket fans actually play cricket, and even most of these stopped
playing it years ago, around the time they left school or college. This

---

[45] Doniger 278.

does not, however, diminish their appreciation of and involvement in cricket. One can discuss the limits of their understanding of a square cut or a googly, but this too is not a barrier between them and cricket. They can enjoy it passively, and they enjoy it massively. This can be said of all sports, with the partial exception of something like chess, though even a chess game can be appreciated by a spectator with only a rudimentary knowledge of the rules of the game and no active desire to 'play' it. This cannot be said at all of literature as literature. There is no passive involvement in literature. Not only does it require the rudimentary ability to read, but, above all, the effort to read with deep attention to the intricacies of that particular text. Even music and art can be appreciated passively to a certain degree. One does not need to know anything about painting in order to appreciate, even be deeply invested in, Rembrandt's or Picasso's paintings. True, one does not need to be a writer in order to appreciate literature, but the required activity of reading—as the word 'activity' implies—cuts off any avenue to passive enjoyment. Reading literature is not a passive matter, and, hence too, it is constantly a matter of evaluation and judgement. It demands not belief or disbelief, which are simple matters and grossly distort the reality 'out there' and 'in here', but agnosticism.

Conclusion: A Call to Literature

The positivist, who is also a fundamentalist of sorts, scoffs: What use is literature in a world of empirical sciences? Usually, we in the fields of literature wriggle out of answering this question by painfully parsing the limits of 'use'. Or we seek refuge behind political, social, psychological, cognitivist, and other—'harder'—readings, which often, though not always, fail to address anything distinctive about literature, making, for example, a 'historical novel' seem to be just the lazy person's access to 'history'. From there, 'everything goes' is a short slide.

But the question does not go away, also because it is a question about the 'arts' in general. Its relentless impact can be observed more closely in fields that cultivate 'scientific' methods, such as social studies and history. In the case of the latter, for instance, at least from the time of the German historian Leopold von Ranke, there has been a tendency to move history away from literature and philosophy and closer to the methodological and empirical premises of the sciences. The debate whether history is a science or not raged throughout the nineteenth century and entered the twentieth century too, with only the rare historian, such as G. M. Trevelyan, championing history as an 'art'. Mostly historians have discussed to what extent history can be a science rather than to what extent it is an 'art'. There they have run into, and honestly acknowledged, various problems; among them, this essential one, as formulated by E. H. Carr: Science can be used to predict events, but does that apply to history?[1]

The answers to this have been varied, and I will avoid all of them, because I consider the question misleading. Prediction means telling what can happen in a future that is essentially different from the past and the present. One does not 'predict' that boiling an egg in water for three minutes will result in a hard-boiled egg. But contrary

[1] E. H. Carr, *What is History?* London: Penguin Books, 1990 (1961).

Literature Against Fundamentalism. Tabish Khair, Oxford University Press. © Tabish Khair (2024).
DOI: 10.1093/oso/9780198919582.003.0007

to what is assumed, the sciences do not predict in that sense: they essentially boil a known egg in known waters. It appears to be a prediction in the humanities because the material that the sciences work with and on change very slowly. The human DNA today is essentially the same as it was 5,000 years ago; trees have essentially the same structure that they had 100,000 years ago; viruses, despite their frequent mutations, are structured in the same way as they were a million years ago; chemical properties and gravity have not changed for billions of years; the essential structures of atoms seem, at least in our experience of the universe, unchanging across time and space. The predictive properties of science seem remarkable because they are not predictions, in the *human* sense of the term: one would need to 'predict' gravity only if the factors determining it changed every few years or in different countries. At times, true, they are inferences, but these inferences are based on factors that stay unchanging, principles and laws that stay the same because we are essentially looking at the same material and factors. In particular, I suspect, the periodic table seems to haunt the minds of humanities scholars—because it was used to predict chemical elements that were yet to be discovered. But once the periodic law was discovered the rest followed mechanically: it was not a prediction in that sense. The chemical elements, unlike, say, the words of a language, were not capable of any change on their own, any eccentric change beyond the periodic law.

The humanities work with constantly changing factors. Economic structures, cultures, societies, languages, all are in constant throes of change. My students have trouble understanding Shakespeare's English, and Old English is called English simply because of national reasons, because it is as different from current English as Sanskrit is from Hindi. Here we are talking of a surviving and codified 'national' linguistic trajectory over just a few centuries. The subjects of study of the humanities change far more and far more quickly than the subjects of study of the sciences. The human desire for universality and permanence—and, hence, one of the incentives for a God—might well be the outcome of this largely overlooked factor: human existence is among the most quickly and constantly changing of all existences. It changes many billion times faster than the universe. Need it be pointed out that existence for human beings is not just a matter of genetic material wrapped in protein, and hence its changes cannot be tallied only in terms of mutations? To expect the humanities to 'predict' the future in, say, twenty years is far more extreme than expecting Newton's physical laws to apply verbatim in the realm of quantum physics.

In his study, *The Structure of Scientific Revolutions*, Thomas S. Kuhn illustrates how science is a more selective and less coherent affair than is commonly assumed. Kuhn does not adopt the relativist stance of dismissing the achievements of science as just another story amongst many. Instead, he looks at how science has developed—though 'develop' is not the right word, for among the things he highlights is the fact that the self-narrative of science, like all self-narratives, is written *after* the event. The decisive 'event' here is a change of paradigm, which he illustrates with the metaphor of a 'gestalt switch': for instance (at its simplest), when the lines on the paper that one saw as a duck suddenly reveal themselves to be a rabbit. Unlike an ordinary gestalt switch, a change of paradigm, for instance, from Galilean physics to Newtonian physics, is a much more 'exclusive' matter, as the world 'changes' for good once the switch is made. In some ways, so to say, it is no longer desirable or maybe even possible to see those lines as a duck once again. Instead, all those elements in the past—as well as all the unresolved matters ('problems' or 'crises') in the present—are constructed in accordance to the new paradigm. As Kuhn notes, '[t]he result is a persistent tendency to make the history of science look linear or cumulative, a tendency that even affects scientists looking back at their own research'.[2]

Whatever literature might or might not be, science is neither as coherent, as cumulative, and as 'positive' in its knowledge claims as we assume, particularly in those areas of the humanities that want desperately to achieve the condition of science in order to bask in its greater prestige. This is not to say that the 'knowledge claims' of science are just tall stories; it is to situate them within given paradigms which do not just explain certain matters better, but, as Kuhn repeatedly highlights, also determine what we are looking at and what questions we are asking (or not asking). In other words, a paradigm is structured

---

[2] Thomas S. Kuhn, *The Structure of Scientific Revolutions*, first published 1962 (Chicago and London: The University of Chicago Press, 2012), 138.

by the material it is looking at: Newton and Einstein look at slightly different material.

Kuhn calls science done *within* a paradigm 'normal science'. This is science that is basically concerned with plugging the holes in the paradigm and solving its accredited 'problems', often under pressure from a competing paradigm. At best, the scientist working within a paradigm tests the problems within it; she does not test the rules of the game. She does not step outside its material limitations.

Normal science, Kuhn illustrates, is good at solving its accredited problems, but far less capable of overcoming the unresolved—and some irresolvable—'crises' within it. Such a solution takes place only with a paradigm change, which introduces a slightly different way of looking at the same 'facts', a slightly different set of questions to be asked of 'reality', so much so that, Kuhn notes, in effect the world changes just a bit. Every new paradigm solves some crucial problems better, but it also looks at the world differently: that is one of the reasons it solves the crises that the previous paradigm had been unable to resolve. However, this shift is also one of the reasons why, until the new paradigm takes over for a number of reasons, adherents of the older paradigm(s) consider the newcomer to be essentially mistaken in its approach and results.

Why have I offered this paraphrase—unfortunately shorn of the complexity and details of Kuhn's book—of the way science operates, as against how we see it as operating? The reason is simple. Science, like literature, is not dealing directly with the reality out there. It is finding ways to see, shape, and talk about that reality. Please note that this does not assume that there is no 'reality' out there, or that all ways of talking about or studying that reality are relative or equivalent constructs. However, Kuhn makes a pertinent point about contemporary philosophers of science, most of whom no longer 'seek absolute criteria for the verification of scientific theories'.[3] This is so because no theory can be exposed to all possible relevant tests and hence 'verified', once and for all. Instead, philosophers of science discuss the probability of a theory in the light of the evidence that exists. There can, in that sense, be better and more accurate theories, at least in the given context and with the available evidence. To use a banal example from

[3] Ibid., 144.

literature, it is more probable that Twain's *Huckleberry Finn* is about identity, race, America, etc., than that it is about how to travel by river, or steamboats, or spaceships.

If we juxtapose this discussion of science against what I have said of literature in the book, we come across an aspect I have often highlighted: the relationship of language, even the 'language of numbers', to the 'reality out there'. I have noted how various other uses of language, in fields like law or sociology, try to control this relationship for the sake of accuracy. They do it in two major ways: (a) by demarcating what they are looking at, and (b) by demarcating the 'exact' meaning of their words (terminology, with its concomitant danger of slippage into jargon). Science, by this account, does something similar.

In all these cases, whether from the humanities, the social sciences, or the hard sciences, certain questions are asked and answered, and certain questions cannot be asked or answered. This is in the nature of 'knowledge'. However, as I have repeatedly pointed out in this book, literature refuses this demarcation of the relationship of language to reality. It does so by *not* corralling the noise, gaps, incongruences, and silences in the relationship; it embraces them. It does so by recognizing the limits of language, and in the process going beyond language. If one thinks of Kuhn's normal science as working within the problems of the given paradigm and necessitating a change of paradigm to overcome its 'crises', then, in effect, literature by definition refuses the paramountcy of paradigms. When it works only and solely within the given paradigms—say, that of a given and established genre—it is not literature, as I define it here. But even there the matter is not so simple.

The Roles of Genre

A literary genre is not a paradigm, and yet a lot of what Kuhn says about scientific paradigms applies to it. For instance, the paradigm is prior to rules. Kuhn notes the 'severe difficulty of discovering the rules that have guided particular normal-scientific traditions' and that paradigms depend far less on explicit rules than on 'finger exercise' and related experience-based consensus.[4] Something similar can be

[4] Ibid., 46–7.

said of literary genres. Even though there are literalists, often with a PhD, who list the rules of a genre, in actual fact any strict adherence to a specific set of rules reduces a genre—even the 'literary novel', if considered a genre—to what I call 'pulp'.[5] At best, these generic rules have a historical, or rather topological, significance.

A genre grows and expands in ways that are similar to a scientific paradigm. Working within any given paradigm, 'normal science does not aim at novelties of fact or theory' and instead looks at problems, solved or unsolved, that the paradigm highlights. Individual works within an established genre operate in a similar fashion. The individual detective novel does not step outside the genre, but, if it is good, it looks at 'problems' which are intricate or unusual. That is why a mere repetition of the style of Sir Arthur Conan Doyle is not sufficient to create a 'new' and 'good' detective novel, no matter how many copies it may sell. Such repetition, I suggest, is what marks the difference between genre and pulp. Pulp, like many unbought detective novels or spy thrillers illustrate, is obviously not what sells a lot, and some 'literary novels' sell more than many examples of pulp. Pulp is what does not explore—and, at its best, challenge—the problems and dimensions of the genre. It is like an experiment that holds no scientific value, whatever its pedagogic use, because it has been done ad infinitum. All of us remember such experiments from science classes in high school. They even used to be fun at times.

A good genre novel is like interesting work within a paradigm: it is useful to illustrate and explore the paradigm, and it solves the accredited problems within the paradigm. It is through such reiterative but critical exploration that a paradigm is exceeded or replaced, according to Kuhn. Most of the necessary work, as Kuhn notes, is merely a confirmation of the paradigm, an attempt to solve its hitches and problems without exceeding it, until a crisis or a number of crises are thrown up by such work. It is only then that we are forced to step into another paradigm, because the previous paradigm can simply not resolve those crises.

[5] For me, a 'literary novel' is essentially pulp if it replicates the turgidity and difficulty associated with some great 'literary novels' simply for effect and without the requirement, need, or ability to go beyond what can be said in language or address other aspects of the 'reality' portrayed.

A genre exists in a similar way: a number of 'normal texts' that explore all the different features of the paradigm, always adding a new 'narrative' (the intellectual detective, the hard-boiled detective, the cop detective, the outside-the-system cop, etc.), until finally we reach a work that takes up a 'narrative situation' that exceeds the genre. And in that moment we have the possibility of a new genre coming into being. At the risk of sounding bathetic, let us take as example the intergalactic cop. The genre that comes up then is obviously not just detective fiction.

I am trying to suggest that in generic terms too literature can be seen as a thinking device. It is when this thinking is suspended and turned into rote production that we can talk of pulp, and in that sense both a detective novel and a literary novel can be pulp. Kuhn also illustrates the movements of science using another metaphor: he suggests there is a 'parallelism between puzzles and the problems of normal science'.[6] He notes that a puzzle needs more than one possible solution, and at the same time it assumes rules that 'limit both the nature of acceptable solutions and the steps by which they are to be obtained'.[7] Once again, pulp is a puzzle that has been done a million times: like those small boxes we buy in airport shops to while time away during a vacation. A good 'genre' text is more than that: while it works with acceptable solutions and given steps, it nevertheless allows for greater challenge. But a great work of literature is a puzzle that, to some extent, changes the acceptable solution and/or given steps. To think of genre as a predetermined and fixed box is to miss the point about literature—and even about literary genres.

Specialisation, Thinking, and Jargon

However, to say all this is not to posit a teleological reading of the history of literature. Such a reading would be rightly scoffed by any decent reader. Who can contend that literature has necessarily grown better with the ages? While the argument that it has grown worse is just as unsustainable, it would be a rash person—and a bad reader—who would claim that the plays being written today are better than

6 Ibid., 38.
7 Ibid.

those written by Shakespeare or Kalidasa, that the short stories of the best living writers exceed those by Chekhov or Saadat Hasan Manto, or that our living poets have developed a form of poetry superior to the works of William Blake or Emily Dickinson. We need not even talk of the Greek classics, which, to certain secular critics in the West, are the closest literary equivalent to revealed texts, and just as fraught with danger in discussion.

This is obviously a glaring difference between 'thinking' in literature and 'thinking' in science. Most of us are fairly convinced—and there is good evidence to hold such a conviction—that science has 'progressed' over the years. Most of us will be willing to accept that the best scientists in the world today are 'better' than the best scientists in the world during the Elizabethan Age. Why this difference? Why is it that if literature is a thinking device, it seems to show no, or far less, cumulative effect than science? Once again, I will return to Kuhn to clarify this point, apart from stressing, as noted earlier, that if you are looking at essentially unchanged 'material' and 'rules', then the cumulative effect of simply gathering information and/or knowledge will inevitably seem to be a progress.

Kuhn makes another point. He draws a crucial distinction between the sciences and other disciplines, though he puts some, like the social sciences and psychology, somewhere in between. He notes that the sciences are not judged outside their fields. This is not to say that the sciences are not affected by, say, constraints of funding which are obviously also a matter of public opinion and political fads. What he points out is a simpler matter: only physicists can pass judgement over the theory of relativity or quantum theory. Relativity and quantum theory are not good examples, and they are paradigmatic theories. One can think of something smaller, more precise—a problem within a given paradigm. When a biologist publishes a paper it is judged by biologists; when an experiment is devised in chemistry it is checked by experts in the field of chemistry; and so on. Actually, the specialization is even more precise: we are talking of experts within a specific field, be it biology or chemistry. While the greatest figures in a field might cross sub-sections, and sometimes even fields (hence the academic cant about 'multidisciplinarity', 'interdisciplinarity', etc.), most, say, physicists, would work in specialized sub-sections like quantum physics, solid-state physics, high-energy physics, etc. It is their peers in these specialized sub-sections who are 'addressed' by their work, and who pronounce on it. Kuhn goes so far as to say that typically such specialized scientific communities might contain 'perhaps one hundred members, occasionally significantly fewer'.[8]

Such specialization lends itself to 'progress'[9]: 'Viewed from within any single community, however, whether of scientists or non-scientists, the result of successful creative work is progress'.[10] The 'truth' of science is a concrete 'fact' as it is minutely demarcated. Progress takes place within these specialized units and it leads to the experience of the progress of the sciences as a whole.

This is not exactly the case in other fields, though Kuhn does not say so. Fields like history, sociology, general philosophy, literature, and others, are open to opinion and judgement from all sides. Some, like sociology or psychology, try to overcome this by constructing methods and terminologies that resemble those of the sciences.[11] And yet, they cannot approach the exact state of the sciences, because by definition their focus cannot be constricted to the kind of increasing specialization that science produces. Reductionism leads only that far in other fields. Even the results of successful reductionism in the other fields remain embedded as part of a larger whole. Kuhn suggests that if we look at the social sciences or even the humanities in terms of highly subdivided and specialized areas within them, we will also see a pattern of 'progress' similar to that of the sciences. The problem is that such 'specialization' and reductionism is self-limiting in the humanities: finally, they have to start looking at the larger whole of society, human behaviour, ecology, etc.

The humanities will always seem to lack progress, compared to the sciences, because of the very nature of their endeavour and concerns. It is in the nature of the humanities to examine 'material' that change rapidly and endlessly. On the other side, it is also in the nature of science to produce results from reductionist approaches, which lead to

[8] Ibid., 177.

[9] It also, by the way, keeps highly specialist terms, used only in these specialist circles, from becoming jargon.

[10] Ibid., 161.

[11] Though the broader a field, the more its terms might tend to turn into jargon.

greater specialization. Such approaches are quickly exhausted of their potential elsewhere. But there is another major problem: language, and language about language.

Now, it is not as if this problem does not exist in the sciences. Let me illustrate this with just one example: that of the DNA. As scholars like Judith Roof and Michel Morange have noted, the general understanding, sometimes also used by scientists, of the DNA is based on misleading metaphors of 'book', 'computer programme', etc. Not only is the DNA a misleading shorthand for 'gene', the complexity of the gene itself is reduced to existing cultural analogies, which Roof lists as 'the code, the book, the alphabet, sentences, words, chapters, histories, the Rosetta stone, the Holy Grail, the recipe, the blueprint, the text, the map, the homunculus, software, and others'.[12] However, behind all these assumptions about the DNA, some inadvertently repeated by scientists, there lies a particular kind of specialized focus, which involves proteins and sugars. Hence, while 'representations of scientific fact are always more than fact',[13] this specialization that returns the working scientist to proteins and sugars is not available to the humanities or even the social sciences. Humanities and the social sciences, despite whatever they do to mimic the sciences, are looking at completely different subject matters.

It can be argued, and at least many in the social sciences and some in the humanities seem to believe so, that the way out is to become like the sciences: divide, subdivide, focus. Is this the way out? Why not, for instance, reduce literary criticism to, say, literary Darwinism. While Darwinism, like any other field relating to humans can be useful in literary studies, it is obvious that to stop at the level of evolutionary theory is to say close to nothing about the literary text—and the world of its writer or readers. Sure, fear has an evolutionary purpose, and we are motivated to fear things that, perhaps, for centuries we have had to avoid: things with fangs and beaks, for instance. What, however, does it tell us about a book that constructs or contends some of the images we 'fear', say, the Turk or the Jew with a hooked nose? And is it enough to say that we like 'horror stories' because fear gives us

---

[12] Judith Roof, *The Poetics of DNA* (Minneapolis: University of Minnesota Press, 2007), 7.

[13] Ibid., 22.

evolutionary advantages, or 'love stories' because of the 'Darwinian' aspects of mating, as some of my students at Aarhus University are unfortunately trained to propose in their thesis statements? In order to engage with a literary text, we will perforce have to go beyond the basic Darwinian facts of our existence. That, unfortunately, is inevitable for a species that is cultural and historical as well as biological. It is even more inevitable when reading something, say, a novel, that is a cultural and historical construct. We need not even talk about what the novel or poem contains or conveys, in and outside language, with and without words, in order to realize this.

Language, I have highlighted, is unavoidable even in the representation of science, though its minute, specialized focus returns the best scientists to evidence that lies beyond language. When they represent this evidence, this 'fact', they run the danger of language once again, but at least the 'fact' is out—or in—there to experiment with: one can, for instance, look at a microbe through powerful lenses, verify quantum effects, test an equation in numbers, etc. Narrow, high specialization keeps science terms from turning into jargon. In all other fields, we are talking about larger spheres of reading and concerns, where no evidence exists entirely outside language: every experimentation of the 'facts' involve language right from the start, and not just when we start explaining the results to others. Even in the sciences, as I have indicated, the slipperiness of language and its reciprocal effects on 'reality' cannot be totally avoided: it can only be bracketed, with very close subdivision and delimitation of focus, an option not available to the humanities. But to say so is not to say that nothing exists outside language. Language is not the only thing that exists for us. How does one deal with that situation? I have argued throughout this book that one deals with it through literature: a mode or ethos of reading as thinking that recognizes and works this problem.

Something out There and in Here

Finally, what I say about literature can be critiqued on the same grounds that the new atheists could bring to any mystical defence of God. The mystical defence of God is based on two elements, both of which involve subjectivity. God is either a subjective experience, something to be felt but not communicated, or God is a subjective experience that some have and can manage to communicate, to an extent, to the less attuned. Both are problematic positions, though far superior to the bureaucratization of Divinity and faith that all established religions—and most of their offshoots—enable. Established religions, in that sense, approach God a bit like how many nineteenth-century liberal humanists approached literature: as a universal, unchanging Truth that needs to be 'taught' to humankind. Belief in the right God, enabled by the bureaucratic channels of accredited rituals and unbending textual guidelines, is what is sought to be achieved, just as traditional liberal humanism often assumed that the end purpose of literature was to cultivate the habit of 'correctly' reading a set of canonical texts.

On the other hand, the mystical position on God shares much with relativism and contains all its weaknesses. Two in particular: (a) if God is a subjective experience, we can never discuss or agree on it, and, hence, we are finally left with the options of not talking about it or arbitrarily insisting on our specific experience; and (b) if God is a subjective experience available to a few highly refined souls, who can then, if we listen and obey and trust, provide access to the rest of us, then again we are back to a relationship of arbitrary power, the *guru–shishya* (master–disciple) ethos. This second position, in effect, shares also with the traditional belief in individual genius, which sees great writing as the emanation of great minds, and essentially expects the rest of us to cultivate the ability to hail and agree with these great minds.

As against these positions, I have formulated a concept of God as a function of thinking in language. This, I have suggested, is different from both faith in God and the new atheistic dismissal of God. Instead, I have asked how human beings could even begin to conceptualize their difference without having a concept like God at one level, just as they distinguished themselves from 'animals' at another level. This, as I have suggested, happens because the experience of being human cannot be totally captured in language and because language also penetrates and sometimes alters all that we experience. This can also be said of existence in general. Fundamentalist and established religious approaches evade this problem, by pinning down God to the language of rituals, tutelage, and conviction. By pinning down 'God', they essentially pin down 'human'—killing two impossible birds with one stone.

It is in this sense that I have argued, here and elsewhere, that fundamentalists commit the greatest 'blasphemy' against God: what is it but blasphemy, in *religious* terms, when you pin down what, even in your canonical religious texts, you concede is beyond human experience and language? Iconoclastic religions, like Wahhabi Islam, do not manage to get out of this conundrum by outlawing any physical depiction of Divinity, because they still need language to talk about it. Hence, for instance, the many names of Allah, all of which, such as kindness and mercy, are human attributes and can only be understood in terms of limited human experience. Idols can be erected in language too. Actually, all uses of human (abstract) language in established religion contain an element of idolatry—talking of an inaccessible reality in terms of human metaphors.[14]

The 'abstract' in my definition of language is, to some extent, similar to what Harari considers 'fiction': 'The ability to speak about fictions is the most unique feature of Sapiens language'.[15] He correctly adds that 'as far as we know, only Sapiens can talk about entire kinds of entities that they have never seen, touched or smelled'.[16] But Harari's version shares, to my mind, a bit of the safety of a post-postmodern understanding of language, which stops at the correct perception that there are no positive terms undergirding the (necessary or unnecessary, useful or disastrous) fictions that human language creates: 'There are no gods [. . .], no nations, no money, no human rights, no laws and no justice outside the common imagination [fiction] of human beings' (Harari, p. 31). In my reading of what literature does as literature, I do not restrict 'imagination' to fiction in the small sense of what does not exist objectively, but also extend it to contemplation, in the larger sense of an ability to think about what does not or does not seem to exist objectively which has a constitutive impact on what does exist

[14] One can write a book, or at least an essay, tracing how my notion of the concept of God runs parallel to the religious notion of God as being beyond description, understanding, experience, etc., as I have suggested earlier. In other words, both on the side of atheism and belief there is this shared space, just as both on the side of atheism and belief there is a completely mistaken attempt to dismiss and define 'God', respectively. This needs to be noted, because if the former space enables a conversation, the latter only allows arguments at best.

[15] Harari, *Sapiens*, 27.

[16] Ibid.

as 'object'.[17] One illustration that runs throughout this book centres around the 'fiction', in Harari's words, of 'God': it is a fiction that, as illustrated earlier, leads to a (re)definition of the 'human' too. The 'fiction' of 'God'—as is the case with all fiction in literature when read as literature—does not stand alone in a subjective void; it arises from and effects the 'objective' world of which it is both a constituted and a constituting aspect.

I am not making the claim that an author has such superior vision that it enables them to see into far spaces. Without denying individual aspects like empathy, complex cultural backgrounds, sensitivity to difference brought about by choice or circumstances, and acute critical thinking on the part of authors, I am not constructing the author along the lines of a mystical sage. In short, I am not arguing that Joseph Conrad in *Heart of Darkness* or Twain in *Huckleberry Finn* was essentially above the cultural prejudices of his age, that somehow his language had cast aside the dross of his society and flapped away into ethereal universality. It is true that some authors might create significant literature by consciously pressing against the prejudices or convictions of their age. This could be the result of political convictions, or of their otherness, say, in terms of race or gender or sexuality, to the mainstream culture. But even here, as one can see in George Orwell's *1984*, there is the more difficult achievement of contesting the limits of language. It is this that matters. There is always a difference between reportage and literature, even when the latter contains the former, a difference that is obscured when literature is read solely as effective communication or when Western critics celebrate non-Western literature as a kind of native reportage.

Literature, I have argued, is the result of contemplative contestation, born from the awareness that language is necessary and vital,

[17] If language enables fictions that unite humans beyond the band-limits of 100 or 150 individuals, as Harari notes, such as by positing a god or a nation, it also, as Harari remarks (but does not discuss as much), leads to an endlessness of fictions, some of them likely to be inimical to others. What he is etching in reasoned language is essentially not too far from the religious myth of the tower of Babel. What he is alluding to are the many political, religious, and other conflicts that afflict us. Hence, language, because it both enables and disables, cannot simply be the evolutionary force that Harari and others consider it to be—if it does nothing else but enable fictions. Hence, my preference for terms like 'contemplation' over terms like 'fiction' to describe the capacity of (abstract) language.

but not enough. Literature does not evade or blanket this awareness, as is the tendency in all other disciplines. It works with this awareness. And, hence, literature uses not just the possibilities of language, but also what can be called noise and silence. Great literature is not written by great minds that can look into the future. Great literature is written by highly skilled wordsmiths who are aware, consciously or not, of this mutual relationship of language and reality. This might be enabled by a different experience of reality too, but this difference is not sufficient on its own, or all 'misfits', adventurers and travellers would have written literature.

There is an impetus towards fundamentalism in any field that aims at talking about 'reality' in language: both the option of total clarity and absolute obscurity lead to fundamentalist positions. Literature avoids both these options. Culler means something similar when he notes that a literary work 'presents itself as exemplary but simultaneously declines to define the range or scope of that exemplarity'.[18] This, I argue in this book, it does not do solely through language: it does so also through silence, gaps, noise, contradiction, paradox, irony, and many other modes that essentially run against the notion of language as transparently communicable. There are two sides to this endeavour: the first one consists of *facing up* to the existence of silence, gaps, noise in limiting language about 'reality', in 'us' or 'out there', and the other one of *using* silence, gaps, noise etc. to overcome some of these limits.

The complexity of this endeavour can be illustrated with reference to a famous literary essay: Chinua Achebe's critique of Joseph Conrad's *Heart of Darkness* (1899). In his essay, Achebe had not just called the novella a racist one, but even accused Conrad of racism.[19] In a chapter of my book, *The Gothic, Postcolonialism and Otherness*, I spent some time showing how, despite Achebe's valid objections to the text and the historically racist context of *Heart of Darkness*, Conrad's novella does something much more—and it does so through a very complex use of the gaps, silences, and noises of and in its own words. For instance, the image of a bloodthirsty idol that demands a sacrifice is used

[18] Jonathan Culler, *The Literary in Theory*, 33.

[19] Chinua Achebe, 'An Image of Africa: Racism in Conrad's 'Heart of Darkness', *Massachusetts Review*, vol. 18 (1977), 782–94.

not to illustrate Africa, though the notion informs it, but to 'justify' European colonization and civilization. Similarly, while Africans are dubbed cannibals, the very category of 'cannibal' is thrown open to doubt: What does it mean when starving 'cannibals', despite their superior numbers, do not attack and presumably eat the Europeans at their mercy? There are too many episodes in the novel of the realities of oppressive colonization being partly narrated and then politely evaded—as when a massacre of Africans by Europeans is eluded by the text as 'lost in [gun]smoke'. The novella, finally, ends in a famous lie[20]—uttered by the white narrator to a young white woman in Brussels—which I, and others, have defined as the lie of civilization. It is a lie of civilization because the narrator and the woman have to participate in it in order to keep up their pretence of civilization, which involves avoiding the reality of European actions in Africa. In some ways, the language that they have about themselves and others does not allow anything apart from this final lie to be brought out of Africa. It is immaterial whether the full import of this lie is intentional on the part of the narrator or the author, or if it is the consequence of the language used: the fact that it can today be read as a 'lie of colonialism' or 'lie of civilisation', and not just a lie of civility, indicates that the text of *Heart of Darkness* has exceeded the limits of the language of its age.

Given these and many other elements, I indicated in my book that Achebe partly fails to read *Heart of Darkness*, because he focusses on its words, words that, given its time (1899), were inevitably racist. Writing in the second half of the twentieth century, post-colonization, Achebe could see the implicit racism of the language that Conrad had to use to 'narrate' Africa to a white readership, including himself. (What other 'language' about Africa did Conrad have access to in the late nineteenth century?) However, interestingly, Achebe's critique is *not* a fundamentalist one. That is so because when Achebe pointed out the inherent racism of Conrad's words in *Heart of Darkness*, this matter had not been adequately faced up to in Western academia.

---

[20] Essentially, in answering Kurtz's betrothed in Brussels, the narrator, a decent man, gives her the answer she wants: telling her that Kurtz's last words were her name and not 'the horror, the horror' that the narrator can still hear reverberating in his ears in this European capital.

Various universalist readings were being provided, eluding the fact that Conrad's language and depiction of Africans was *also* problematic. It is this critical silence that Achebe heard, and he rightly wrote about and against it; in effect, blaming Conrad for it. This too is an aspect of literature, and the agnostic reading it inculcates.

Achebe also participates, inevitably, in a critical and theoretical development of his own age. Theory, as we know, has put the final nails in the coffins of three assumptions usually attributed to liberal humanism: 'that the meaning of an utterance or text is what the speaker "had in mind", [. . .] that writing is an expression whose truth lies elsewhere, in an experience or a state of affairs which it expresses, [. . .] that reality is what is "present" at a given moment'.[21] I am not trying to resuscitate the dead here. The problem is that the meaning of a text was *never* what the speaker had in mind, and neither did the meaning of writing lie elsewhere, because it was already being done in language. Language assumes both contestation and sharing. I cannot even opine about what the writer of a text in Chinese 'had in mind' as I do not know Chinese. But I might do so with a text in English, Hindi, or Danish, which I can read. However, in each of these cases, a language that I 'know' will come to me differently, inflected not only by where it is coming from but also who it is coming to. For instance, as I have discussed in an essay, when I was made to memorize William Wordsworth's 'I Wondered Lonely as a Cloud' (1807) in my school in small-town India, I had no idea what daffodils looked or smelled like. This obviously made me read the poem a bit differently. This is a middling example. We can dredge up far more complicated ones. But the point I am making is that the very nature of language, and then the very nature of writing, as I have explored in a chapter, imposes a large degree of uncertainty on any claim about what the speaker 'had in mind' or the expression of truth behind any piece of writing. More than that, as language predates the 'speaker' and the text, this uncertainty has already been encountered and differently navigated by the speaker and the text in the first instance too. Hence, reality is never 'present' at a given moment, and all good literature knows it—both in its writing down and in its reading up. Literature works with the

---

[21] Jonathan Culler: *Literary Theory: A Very Short Introduction*. Oxford: Oxford University Press, 1997 (2000), 4.

absences too: hence, its employment of silence, noise, contradiction, ambiguity, etc.

A writer of literature does not, being aware of the material of the construction of 'literature' and the forest of its siting, work with the kind of notion of transparency of language that would present the speaker's mind, or 'truth', or the present/reality as something just outside a window of clear glass. And no adequate reader peers through such a clear pane of glass either. However, the window remains there, and it shows certain things, occludes others. It points in a certain direction. Neither the view nor the frames are chosen haphazardly, and no matter what readers do, they have to look through that particular window, with its many and selective vistas, but not a careless, mindless eternity of sights. As James Bridle notes in a different, but not unrelated, context, '[t]hat which we see shapes not just what we think, but how we think'.[22]

In short, there is something out there and in here. Throughout this book, I have not operated with a fixed or given or even an entirely knowable idea of reality, and neither have a treated language as a clear window to it. But I have assumed that something—'reality' that is always liable to be contested and never fully knowable—does exist 'out there' and 'in here'. Without getting into an elaborate discussion that shades from philosophy to sophistry, I claim (and I am not alone in this claim) that the real is what also exists outside your mind. It is in that sense that we can discuss whether a ghost, a problem, a unicorn, or an elephant is real or not. Of course, as the real cannot exist at all for you unless it exists in your mind too, and as its existence inside and outside your mind, and the relationships thereof, cannot even be discussed without involving your mind, the existence of the real is never just an exterior matter. It is also always a matter of language, for one. But because the real cannot exist for me and for you outside our minds and our languages does not mean that it does not exist—a matter that can be tested in many ways, including for instance, in a third mind or language. Literature, one can argue, comes into existence in the space of such testing, and the gaps thereof, for it assumes both reality and the reality of language and exists as a

[22] James Bridle, *New Dark Age: Technology and the End of the Future*. London: Verso, 2018 (2019), 19.

constant interrogation of its nature—an interrogation that is repeated, and repeated with potential differences, every time a work of literature gains another reader. There is no author of a literary work in at least this sense, if by author we mean just one person.

'[V]entriloquism is a two-way street', notes Wendy Doniger, when talking of the overwhelming presence of men and Brahmins in the authorship of classical Sanskrit texts.[23] What she means is not that different from Plato's reasons for suspicion of the poet: the texts, though written mostly by Brahmin men, do not just try, despite obvious limits, to sometimes feature 'others', but, more significantly, the ideas of others might have unwittingly gotten into the head of the Brahmin male author. Or, as Amitav Ghosh gets a character to suggest in *The Calcutta Chromosome*, you don't always know who is talking. Hence, right from the start, the reading of literature requires a hermeneutics of subtlety, which is more complex than and very different from the hermeneutics of suspicion that recent theory is (often wrongly) accused of fostering. Actually, a hermeneutics of suspicion is what we grant to any utterance, any use of language: we always question the motivations of the speaker or writer, consciously or subconsciously. Why did she say so? What did she really mean? Does he mean what he said? To reduce the reading of literature to simply the so-called hermeneutics of suspicion is to let it stay at the level of any language use. What literature calls for and trains us to practice is the hermeneutics of subtlety—which demands multiple readings, some across one another, and which combines the transparent meanings of words with what has not been said or cannot be said, combines legitimate sound with silence and noise. In that sense, we are always agnostic when we read literature as literature.

A lingering question that might be bothering the reader, especially one of an academic bent, is whether what I call the agnostic reading demanded by literature is an aspect of the text or of the reader. The short answer, as adumbrated throughout this book, is: neither-both. A text where language is ordered by the disciplinary demands of fixity and expectations of absolute correspondence with 'reality'— whether it is a medical tract or a didactic poem—does not lend itself to an agnostic reading as much as *literature* does. No reader can do too

---

[23] Doniger, 37.

much with such a text, without doing serious violence to it.[24] Similarly, a reader not willing or used to reading literature as literature is perfectly capable of turning not just the *Book of Job*, but even Shakespeare's *King Lear* or Samuel Beckett's *Waiting for Godot* into a flat, transparent, fundamentalist text about, say, faith.

Yes, traditional literary scholarship, like established religion, was wrong about the need to teach people the *ritual* of reading the right texts. Even the greatest literary texts cannot teach a reader anything, including that much-celebrated attribute of empathy these days, if they are reduced to rituals, which by definition serve as anodyne to the necessary pain of thinking. Evelyn Waugh gets this precisely in his story, 'The Man Who Liked Dickens' (1933), which presents a man moved to tears by the novels of Charles Dickens, read out ritualistically to him, but unable or unwilling to empathize with the only other human being on his island. If empathy cannot be gained from the ritual of reading literature, then we cannot even take matters like ethics or morality as engrained in literature *per se*. It is not what literature tells you that is the crucial element. It is the active process, mode, ethos of reading that literature demands of you that matters. It is this ethos of reading that enables a distinctive kind of contemplation.[25] And this depends on various factors, including material ones, such as your 'reading device', of which, to date, the book remains unmatched—or, maybe, as some recent research has shown, there is a difference in the degree of contemplation even in the simple action of turning the page, in a book or on Kindle, and of scrolling up and down. Of course, this ethos of reading, once cultivated, can be brought to some extent to any activity that involves thinking in language. It is in this sense that literature—and reading literature *as* literature—is an antidote to fundamentalism. Hence, in our age, my argument in this book is also *a call to literature*.

---

[24] Of course, there is nothing, *per se*, that prevents readers, if they want, from reading a medical tract as a message from aliens or God. Though such 'games'—and hence the concept of literature as just play—are games only for people who can escape consequences in the real world, or who mostly gain from them. Even bombing a population can be implicitly portrayed as a 'game'—and sometimes is in the global media, such as CNN, with their recourse to maps, charts, and military experts. Watching Gaza being bombed, as I finish editing this book, it appears doubtful to me that the bombed experience it as a game.

[25] And, hence again, contemplation is an activity, not the passive recourse to 'nothingness' that leisured concepts of 'meditation' mostly turn it into.

Bibliography

Abrams, M. H. and Harpham, G. G., *A Glossary of Literary Terms* (Stamford, CT: Cengage Learning, 2015).

Achebe, Chinua, 'An Image of Africa: Racism in Conrad's "Heart of Darkness"', *Massachusetts Review*, vol. 18 (1977), 782–94.

Adams, Hazard, Ed., *Critical Theory Since Plato*. Revised edition (Fort Worth, TX: Harcourt Brace Jovanovich College Publishers, 1992).

Adleman, Daniel and Vanderwees, Chris, *Psychoanalysis and the New Rhetoric: Freud, Burke, Lacan, and Philosophy's Other Scenes* (London and New York: Routledge, 2022).

Apter, Emily, *The Translation Zone: A New Comparative Literature* (Princeton and Oxford: Princeton University Press, 2006).

Bakhtin, M. M., *The Dialogic Imagination*. Ed. Michael Holquist, trans. Caryl Emerson and Michael Holquist (Austin, TX: University of Texas, 1981).

Barry, Peter, *Beginning Theory: An Introduction to Literary and Cultural Theory*, first published 1995 (Manchester and New York: Manchester University Press, 2009).

Barthes, Roland, 'The Death of the Author', in Roland Barthes, *Image, Music, Text*, trans. by Stephen Heath (London: Fontana Press, 1977), 142–8.

Bassnett, Susan, *Comparative Literature: A Critical Introduction* (Oxford: Blackwell, 1993).

Boehmer, Elleke, *Colonial and Postcolonial Literature* (Oxford: Oxford University Press, 1995).

Bressler, Charles E., *Literary Criticism: An Introduction to Theory and Practice*, first published 1994 (New Jersey: Prentice Hall, 2003).

Bridle, James, *New Dark Age: Technology and the End of the Future* (London: Verso, 2018).

Brontë, Emily, *Wuthering Heights*, first published 1847, ed. A. Lewis (New York: W. W. Norton and Company, 2019).

Carr, E. H., *What is History?*, first published 1961 (London: Penguin Books, 1990).

Cicero, *The Nature of the Gods*, first published 1997, trans. P. G. Walsh (Oxford: Oxford University Press, 2008).

Clark, Katerina and Holquist, Michael, *Mikhail Bakhtin* (Cambridge; MA: Harvard University Press, 1984).

Colebrook, Clare, *Irony* (London: Routledge, 2003).

Chambers, Claire, *British Muslim Fictions: Interviews with Contemporary Writers* (Houndmills and New York: Palgrave Macmillan, 2011).

Chekhov, Anton, *Best Short Stories of Anton Chekhov*, first published 1886, trans. Constance Garnett (Ahmedabad and Mumbai: Jaico Publishing House, 2018).

Conrad, Joseph, *Heart of Darkness and Other Tales*, first published 1899, Ed. Cedric Watts (Oxford: Oxford University Press, 1990)

Culler, Jonathan, *The Literary in Theory* (Stanford: Stanford University, Press, 2007).

Culler, Jonathan, *Literary Theory: A Very Short Introduction* (Oxford: Oxford University Press, 1997).

Davis, Philip, *Reading and the Reader* (Oxford: Oxford University Press, 2013).

Derrida, Jacques, *Of Grammatology*. Trans. by Gayatri Spivak (Baltimore and London: Johns Hopkins University Press, 1976).

Dillet, Benoit; Porter, Robert, and Mackenzie, Iain, Eds. *The Edinburgh Companion to Poststructuralism* (Edinburgh: Edinburgh University Press, 2013).

Doniger, Wendy, *The Hindus: An Alternative History* (Oxford: Oxford University Press, 2009).

Eagleton, Terry, *Literary Theory: An Introduction* (Oxford and Cambridge: Blackwell, 1983).

Eagleton, Terry, *After Theory* (London: Penguin Books, 2004).

Eagleton, Terry, *Holy Terror* (Oxford: Oxford University Press, 2005).

Farkas, Johan and Schou, Jannick, *Post-Truth, Fake News and Democracy: Mapping the Politics of Falsehood* (London and New York: Routledge, 2019).

Felch, Susan M., ed., *The Cambridge Companion to Literature and Religion* (Cambridge: Cambridge University Press, 2016).

Fish, Stanley, *Is There a Text in This Classroom?* (Harvard: Harvard University Press, 1982).

Foucault, Michel, *Madness and Civilization: A History of Insanity in the Age of Reason*, Trans. by Richard Howard (London: Routledge, 1967/1997), 65–70.

Fukuyama, Francis, *The End of History and the Last Man* (New York: Free Press, 1992).

Ghosh, Amitav, *The Nutmeg's Curse: Parables of a Planet in Crisis* (London and Gurugram: Allen Lane, Penguin Random House, 2021).

Gilbert, Sandra M. and Gubar, Susan, *The Madwoman in the Attic: The Woman Writer and the Nineteenth-century Literary Imagination*, first published 1979 (New Haven: Yale University Press, 2002).

Godfrey-Smith, Peter, *Other Minds: The Octopus and the Evolution of Intelligent Life* (London: William Collins, 2018).

Gray, John, *The Book of Job* (Sheffield: Sheffield Phoenix Press Ltd, 2015)

Gunew, Sneja, Ed., *A Reader in Feminist Knowledge* (London and New York: Routledge, 1991).

Han, Byung-Chul, *The Transparency Society*, first published 2012, trans. Erik Butler (Stanford: Stanford University Press, 2015)

Han, Byung-Chul, *The Expulsion of the Other*. first published 2016, trans. Wieland Hoban (Cambridge and Medford: Polity, 2018).

Han, Byung-Chul, *The Scent of Time*, first published 2009, trans. Daniel Steuer (Cambridge and Medford: Polity, 2017).

Harari, Yuval Noah, *Sapiens: A Brief History of Humankind* (London: Vintage, 2011).

Harris, Jonathan Gil, *The First Firangis: Remarkable Stories of Heroes, Healers, Charlatans, Courtesans & Other Foreigners Who Became Indian* (New Delhi: Aleph Book Company, 2015).

Harrison, Tony, *V. and Other Poems*, first published 1984 (New York: Farrar, Straus and Giroux, 1990).

Hitchens, Christopher, *God Is Not Great: How Religion Poisons Everything* (London: Atlantic Books, 2007).

Iser, Wolfgang, *The Act of Reading: A Theory of Aesthetic Response* (Baltimore and London: The Johns Hopkins University Press, 1978).

Kennedy, Randall, *Nigger: The Strange Career of a Troublesome Word* (New York: Vintage Books, 2003).

Khair, Tabish, *Babu Fictions: Alienation in Contemporary Indian English Novels* (New Delhi and Oxford: Oxford University Press, 2001).

Khair, Tabish, *The Gothic, Postcolonialism, and Otherness: Ghosts from Elsewhere* (Houndmills and New York: Palgrave Macmillan, 2009).

Khair, Tabish, 'Is an Atheistic Defence of God Possible?' *Economic and Political Weekly*, Delhi, vol. 51, no. 14 (2016), 39–43. http://www.jstor.org/stable/44002650.

Khosrokhavar, Farhad, *Jihadist Ideology: The Anthropological Perspective* (Aarhus: Centre of Studies in Islamism and Radicalisation, Aarhus University, 2008).

Kosambi, M.M., *Ancient India: A History of Its Culture and Civilization* (New York: Pantheon Books, 1965).

Kuhn, Thomas S., *The Structure of Scientific Revolutions*, first published 1962 (Chicago and London: The University of Chicago Press, 2012).

Lane, Nick, *Oxygen: The Molecule That Made the World* (Oxford: Oxford University Press, 2009).

Levinas, Emmanuel, *Alterity & Transcendence* (New York: Columbia University Press, 1999).

Levine, Robert S., gen. ed., *The Norton Anthology of American Literature*, shorter ninth edition (New York and London: W. W. Norton & Company, 2017).

Lindqvist, Sven, *'Exterminate All the Brutes': One Man's Odyssey into the Heart of Darkness and the Origins of European Genocide*, first published 1997, trans. Joan Tate (London: Granta, 2002).

Lock, Charles, 'Double Voicing, Sharing Words: Bakhtin's Dialogism and the History of the Theory of Free Indirect Discourse,' in *The Novelness of Bakhtin: Perspectives and Possibilities*, eds. Jørgen Bruhn and Jan Lundquist (Copenhagen: Tusculanum, 2001), pp. 71–87.

Loomba, Ania, *Colonialism/Postcolonialism* (London and New York: Routledge, 1998).

Macfarlane, Robert, *Underland: A Deep Time Journey*, first published 2019 (London: Penguin Random House, 2020).

Macherey, Pierre, *A Theory of Literary Production* (1978), Trans. by Geoffrey Wall (London and New York: Routledge, 2006).

Mernissi, Fatima, *The Veil and the Male Elite: A Feminist Interpretation of Women's Rights in Islam* (New York: Basic Books, 1987).

Moore-Gilbert, Bart, *Postcolonial Theory: Contexts, Practices, Politics* (London: Verso, 1997).

Nasta, Susheila, Ed., *Brave New Words* (London: Myriad 2019).

Moretti, Franco, *Distant Reading* (London: Verso, 2013).

Murray, Les, *Selected Poems* (Manchester: Carcanet, 1986).

Nelson, Cary and Grossberg, Lawrence, Eds., *Marxism and the Interpretation of Culture* (Urbana and Chicago: University of Illinois Press, 1988).

Novy, Marianne, *Shakespeare and Feminist Theory*, first published 2017 (London and New York: The Arden Shakespeare, 2019).

Nussbaum, Martha, *Poetic Justice: The Literary Imagination and Public Life* (Boston: Beacon, 1995).

Nussbaum, Martha, *Anger and Forgiveness: Resentment, Generosity, Justice* (Oxford: Oxford University Press, 2016)

Pappas, Nickolas, 'Plato on Poetry: Imitation or Inspiration?' Philosophy Compass, vol. 7, no. 10 (2012), 669–78.

Paden, William E., *Religious Worlds: The Comparative Study of Religion* (Boston: Beacon Press, 1994).

Pesso-Miquel, Catherine and Stierstorfer, Klaus, Ed., *Burning Books: Negotiations Between Fundamentalism and Literature* (New York: AMS Press, 2012).

Rackin, Phyllis, *Shakespeare & Women*, first published 2005 (Oxford: Oxford University Press, 2013).

Roof, Judith, *The Poetics of DNA* (Minneapolis: University of Minnesota Press, 2007).

Said, Edward, *Culture and Imperialism* (New York: Vintage Books, 1993).

Saleemi, Anjum; Bohn, Ocke-Schwen, and Gjedde, Albert, Eds., *In Search of a Language for the Mind-brain: Can the Multiple Perspectives be Unified?* (Aarhus: Aarhus Universitetsforlag, 2005).

Sartre, J-P, *Words*, first published 1967, trans. Irene Clephane (London: Penguin Books, 2000).

Saussure, Ferdinand de, *Course in General Linguistics*. Eds. Charles Bally and Albert Sechehaye, trans. by Wade Baskin (London: Fontana, 1974).

Sheldrake, Merlin, *Entangled Life: How Fungi make our Worlds, Change our Minds, and Shape our Futures* (London: The Bodley Head, 2020).

Sidahmed, S. and Ehteshami, A., eds, *Islamic Fundamentalism* (Boulder, CO: Westview Press/HarperCollins Publishers, 1996).

Stenger, Victor J., *God: The Failed Hypothesis—How Science Shows That God Does Not Exist* (New York: Prometheus Books, 2008).

Tsing, Anna Lowenhaupt, *The Mushroom at the End of the World: On the Possibility of Life in Capitalist Ruins* (Princeton and Oxford: Princeton University Press, 2015).

Truschke, Audrey, *Culture of Encounters: Sanskrit at the Mughal Court* (New York: Columbia University Press, 2016).

Voloshinov, V.N., *Marxism and the Philosophy of Language*, first published 1929, trans. Ladislav Matejka and I. R. Titunik (Cambridge and London: Harvard University Press, 1996).

Vygotsky, Lev S., *Thought and Language*. Revised and expanded edition. Ed. Alex Kozulin, trans. by Eugenia Hanfmann and Gertrude Vakar (Cambridge, MA: The MIT Press, 2012).

Williams, Raymond, *Culture and Society*, first published in 1958 (London: The Hogarth Press, 1993).

Wimsatt W.K. and Beardsley, Monroe C., *The Verbal Icon: Studies in the Meaning of Poetry*, first published in 1954 (Lexington, KY: University Press of Kentucky, 1982).

Wohlleben, Peter, *The Hidden Life of Trees: What they Feel, How they Communicate* (London: William Collins, 2017).

Wohlleben, Peter, *The Inner Life of Animals: Surprising Observations of a Hidden World* (London: Vintage, 2018).

Wood, James, *How Fiction Works* (London: Picador, 2018).

Yong, Ed., *I Contain Multitudes: The Microbes within Us and a Grander View of Life* (London: Vintage, 2016).

Index